My Incredible Supply Chain Journey… and What You Can Learn From It

By Joseph C. Andraski

Trials, Teamwork, and Triumphs

Table of Contents

Preface

I decided some time ago to put my thoughts and experiences together in a book, with the hope that sharing the road that I have traveled and the challenges I have faced will help smooth the path to success for others in the profession that I love, logistics and supply chain management.

You could sum up the sentiment that moved me to write as "sharing, caring, and giving back."

I believe that *sharing* information, contacts, and ideas is so important, because it makes a solid contribution to the knowledge and understanding of any individual.

Caring means having the best interests and the well-being of others at heart. This doesn't apply to just personal relationships. Developing a caring culture within an organization—one that extends to service providers, customers, and suppliers—will lead to an environment of trust.

Finally, *giving back* is a personal commitment to share your experience and what you have learned. It is an expression of gratitude for a rewarding career and what others have done for you. Some of the many ways you can give back include mentoring a student, providing career advice, and volunteering for an industry association.

For me, writing this book isn't about making money. It's about giving back to the industry, and about recognizing my dear friends in academia and the thought leadership they have provided and continue to provide to me.

That is why I want to tell you about the many experiences and challenges I've had, the way these were addressed, and what I learned from each of them. These experiences made me a better person, at least in some respects. I learned a lot about having compassion for people, and about trying to understand a person and what floats his or her boat. With that in mind, it's easier to find ways to motivate that person and make him or her feel like an important member of the team.

I sincerely believe that it's really about the team, and that people make the difference between good and great. In fact, you'll hear a lot in this book about team building, trust, collaboration, and related subjects— particularly as they were practiced at Nabisco, where I spent most of my career.

I'm fortunate to have a great personal "team" that has stood by me throughout my career. Behind every successful person is a mate who provides the love and support that is absolutely critical to whatever success you achieve. I have been blessed to have Regina, my wife of 52 years and a most outstanding woman in every respect imaginable, at my side. And I am so proud of my accomplished children, Laure Rutter, Gina Gramiak, and Maria Hamberlin, and of my seven grandchildren, George, Joey, Amanda, Kate, Simon, Shane and Wyatt. They are all uniquely talented and more than personable. Love those who love you with a commitment and a passion, and that will carry over to who you are in the profession that you choose to pursue.

I wrote this book in my personal style to communicate as effectively as possible—that is, I wrote as though we're having a conversation, and I'm speaking directly with you. I don't use a lot of metaphors, or go into quoting experts in the field, except when it is directly related to the topic at hand and will help you understand the subject.

So I hope you'll enjoy reading *My Incredible Supply Chain Journey ... and What You Can Learn From It,* and that you'll find the book helpful and will refer to it time and time again. I wish you the very best of luck and success with your career, with your organization, and in the development and effective use of your leadership skills.

Joseph C. Andraski
Founder, Collaborative Energizer LLC
November 2013

Introduction

In the Preface, I explained my motivations for writing this book, specifically, my desire to share some of the knowledge gained through many years of experience. To sum it up in a few words, my hope is that you'll find nuggets of information here that will help you move forward in both your personal and your business life.

Now let's take a look at what to expect in the coming chapters.

CHAPTER 1 is about my personal history, from my childhood in Green Ridge, a rough-and-ready coal mining town in Pennsylvania, and onward to how I got into this profession and came to work at various companies, including Standard Brands and Nabisco. I've also touched on some of the personal challenges I've faced and what I have done professionally since leaving Nabisco.

It might strike some as unusual to include my personal story in a book about business. But I've written this chapter to explain where I came from, and how those experiences shaped the beliefs and determination that have carried me through a career that was never easy but was always rewarding. It's my sincere hope that when you read this chapter you'll consider what you can learn from the experience of "the kid from Green Ridge."

CHAPTER 2 will give you some background for understanding the constantly changing environment that I and the logistics and supply chain organization had to function in. It provides a brief overview of the evolution of Standard Brands, Nabisco Brands, RJR Nabisco, and

KKR Nabisco, while explaining how disruptive the years of mergers and acquisitions were for most of us who worked there. (The constant change and turmoil was such a wild and compelling story that it became the subject of the bestselling book *Barbarians at the Gate* and even a movie based on the book.) I knew some of the high-level executives so I've also offered some comments on their management style and priorities. But even for those I didn't know, it was clear how their attitudes about management affected the business and the employees under them.

A lot of the discussions in this book are framed in relation to what went on in distribution, transportation, and logistics at Standard Brands and the various versions of Nabisco. That's where I spent the majority of my career working with some of the best in the business to build one of the most accomplished organizations in the grocery industry.

CHAPTER 3 will give you an idea of how Nabisco's Integrated Logistics group developed from the roots of Standard Brands' distribution organization and then grew into something new and different. Nabisco's logistics team was an acknowledged leader in developing new and extremely relevant business processes and technologies. There might have been other companies that were making similar progress. But through my involvement with the Grocery Manufacturers Association (GMA), Food Marketing Institute (FMI), and the Efficient Consumer Response initiative (ECR), I was aware of what other companies were doing, and I didn't come across any that came close to achieving the progress we had made.

One of the critical differentiators for the Integrated Logistics organization was technology. Rather than rely entirely on commercially available logistics and supply chain software, the group developed a lot of what we needed ourselves. We were able to do that thanks to creative thinking and some super-talented technical people we were fortunate to have with us. So this chapter looks at some of the business systems and processes that made the company and the logistics organization stand out from the crowd. After that, I cover some aspects of the "rough road" I traveled during the mergers and acquisitions and the changes in direction that occurred while I was at both companies.

In **CHAPTER 4**, I share some observations on managing people and organizations. Certain factors—culture, politics, leadership, trust, communication, team building, and change management—influence the success of any organization, both positively and negatively. These are important considerations for every manager and for those in the trenches who aspire to climb the career ladder. That's why I chose to share some of my thoughts on those topics and also explain how those factors played out at Nabisco and affected our team. Then I finish up with some recommendations on how to build successful teams that are based on my experience.

CHAPTER 5 is about collaboration, a subject that is near and dear to me. I've been passionate about collaborative business practices for many years, and I firmly believe that organizations that value and engage in collaboration achieve substantial benefits their competitors can't touch.

In this chapter I share some of my experiences with collaboration at Nabisco—with customers, external trading partners, and internal functions like marketing, finance, manufacturing, and sales. I also take a look at what makes successful collaboration possible, and how initiatives like Collaborative Planning, Forecasting, and Replenishment (CPFR®) and Efficient Consumer Response paid off at Nabisco—even while the company was in turmoil because of successive mergers and acquisitions. This includes a detailed example of ECR and a CPFR® case study involving the grocery chain Wegmans.

CHAPTER 6 is one I especially enjoyed writing. It's about building a state-of-the-art supply chain management business model. But instead of explaining how to do it, I "take a trip down memory lane" and use the experiences of Standard Brands and Nabisco to help describe the key considerations and enablers for developing a successful SCM business model. Among the areas included are order processing, transportation management, warehouse management, inventory management, information accuracy, and metrics.

One of the things I think you'll find especially informative is an account of IT initiatives during the Standard Brands/Nabisco merger period written by my former colleague Al Yasalonis. Al played a primary role in developing our warehouse management system and Logistics Order Tracking System (LOTS) initiatives. Another interesting section is called "Thinking Outside the Logistics Box," which describes some of the innovative practices that helped Nabisco become a recognized industry leader. I'm sure you'll agree that the Integrated Logistics team's dedication, technical expertise, and ingenuity will be clearly evident in those examples.

Instead of focusing on what's been accomplished in the past, **CHAPTER 7** takes a look into the future. This is where I offer some commentary on item-level radio frequency identification (ILRFID), a technology I believe will have a dramatic impact on supply chain management practices.

ILRFID is a proven technology that will be a true game-changer, not just for retail and apparel, where it's had the biggest impact so far, but also for other business segments. As you'll see, there are plenty of ways to quantify the benefits ILRFID offers in terms of inventory accuracy, in-stocks, store-level productivity, customer satisfaction, and increased sales. I've been involved in promoting the development and use of this technology for a long time, and my belief in its value is only increasing.

CHAPTER 8 recaps some of the reasons why I chose to write this book and share my thoughts and experiences with you. Looking back over my career, I think about the roles people played individually and as part of a logistics team that made incredible accomplishments during so much turmoil. I also tell about an experience I had that showed just how crazy things got during all the changes at Nabisco, and then wrap up with some guidelines that sum up what's most important for anyone who wants to succeed not just in business but also as a manager, a mentor, and a human being. I hope you'll take those suggestions to heart.

The book concludes with some "extras" I hope you'll find useful and interesting. The **AFTERWORD** is a collection of some recommendations—brief nuggets of advice based on what I've seen and experienced over the years. In the **APPENDIX** I've gathered some contributions from friends and former colleagues. This is a real potpourri of information that expands on some of the topics covered in the various chapters. For example, there's an essay on change management by my dear friend Prof. Lloyd Rinehart of the University of Tennessee; a CPFR® case study about West Marine from Larry Smith, senior vice president, planning and replenishment; two case studies about multi-vendor consolidation; reminiscences from former Nabisco colleagues about some of the trials, teamwork, and triumphs we experienced together; and a glossary of terms contributed by my friend and former colleague Tony Galli.

Before we wrap this up, I'd like to take a moment to thank some of the people who supported me in this project and who helped move it along from an idea to the finished product you're reading right now.

Sincere thanks to:

Tony Galli, who spent a lot of time reading the book and offering advice and suggestions.

Lloyd Rinehart, who virtually walked by my side, raising subjects that should be included in the book.

Al Yasalonis, who helped edit and contributed his great knowledge, especially on the technology side.

Peter Rogers, who was a senior executive during his entire career, yet relished the opportunity to work with and help everyone in every organization he ran.

Rick Blasgen, whose willingness to publish this book was so very much appreciated. He constantly provided advice and encouragement that was very important to me.

Mitch Mac Donald, a longtime friend who also provided assistance and encouragement.

Regina Andraski, my dear wife, who has supported me during a long career. She has been a real trooper, enduring the many days I spent on the road and managing our household as I managed my business responsibilities.

All of my Nabisco friends and colleagues, who I considered to be my business "family," and who I could count on through every challenge.

Sue Paulson, who has always been there for me, helping out whenever I asked for assistance.

Toby Gooley, who edited the book and helped to make it all that I wanted it to be.

And finally, I would like to say that this book reflects my personal observations, beliefs, and opinions. I can assure you that I have written from my heart.

Chapter 1: Personal History

While I had a very loving family, I essentially grew up with the opposite of a silver spoon in my mouth—more like a rusty nail! My rough-and-tumble childhood contributed to the development of my personality, and that helped me work through the tough times and find ways to survive and win. While I can't claim to have been wildly successful, to put it all into perspective, I am a kid from Green Ridge, Pa., who faced all kinds of challenges throughout my career and found the chutzpah to overcome the obstacles and leave an enviable track record.

That is why I have chosen to open my heart and share my personal history in this book. I hope that my experiences can have a positive effect on those who are in various stages of their careers.

Adventures (and Misadventures) in a Coal Mining Town

I am the product of a great mother and father, born in the Green Ridge section of Hazle Township, a suburb of Hazleton, Pa. My mom and I lived with her parents while my dad served in the U.S. Army. For most of my early years I was known as Joey Brugger. (Brugger was my grandparents' surname.) I had the pleasure, although I didn't know it at the time, of having the most loving childhood anyone could imagine.

My grandparents just couldn't believe that I did anything wrong because I was their angel. So they hovered over and protected me while my mom did her best with a rather rambunctious child.

My mom was dealing with raising her only child as a single parent, as my father, who was in the Army, was always off to faraway lands. He was with us only for a few weeks at a time, during leaves he could arrange. Bottom line, we were poor, but I didn't realize our financial plight, as I had food, clothes, and the essentials for life. The main drawback was that I never got to know my dad very well, and he was always away for birthdays, holidays, and other events that my friends shared with their fathers.

Green Ridge was essentially a coal mining village, and I remember almost everyone who lived there having someone in the family who worked in the mines. There were families with as many as nine children; others had boys who were serving in the military, with a few youngsters still at home.

My first five years in school were spent in a three-room schoolhouse, with first and second grade in Room 1; third, fourth, and fifth grades in Room 2; and sixth, seventh, and eighth grades in Room 3. Each room had a teacher who taught reading, writing, and arithmetic, one grade at a time. Each room was heated with a large coal stove. The boys from the higher grades were given the "honor" of bringing up buckets of coal from the cellar and taking out the ashes at the end of each day. The teachers were responsible for banking the fires at the end of the day and stoking the smoldering coals in the morning.

I remember Mr. Fultz, my teacher in third, fourth, and fifth grade. He had one arm and a large, bulbous nose. He swept the floors using his one arm, after spreading a green, powdery substance that he used to keep the dust down. The floors were wooden and they showed a lot of wear, having served many classes over the years. Imagine—there were no janitors, no administrative staff, or any of what is found in elementary schools today. The teachers did all the heavy lifting and were expected to teach, too. I think you can get the picture that there was little time for personal counseling or interaction between teacher and students. Corporal punishment for misbehavior was at the discretion of the teacher, with parents always deferring to the teacher's judgment.

Getting back to Mr. Fultz: He comes to mind easily because I knew that he really cared about his students. He came across as a hard-nose, but that was at the beginning of the year, when he set the tone and drew the lines showing that he was the boss. However, as the year went on he showed his softer side and smiled easily during the course of the day.

Once I got in trouble for something that I don't recall, which resulted in a parent-teacher meeting. My mom met with Mr. Fultz, and it was a mostly amicable discussion as I remember. They came to an agreement about how to deal with this tough little son of a gun, who had a lot of potential and promise. I just needed to hunker down and spend more time studying and less time having fun in class. The message was clear, but the feeling I got was that Mr. Fultz really cared and wanted to see me do well. So even though he had some 18 to 22 students of various ages and backgrounds to deal with, Mr. Fultz showed interest in me, and that has been a fond memory ever since.

As we grow up, we build our personal foundation on role models who shape our personalities and help us understand what's important. Mr. Fultz was my first role model, the first person outside my immediate family who showed compassion and interest, with no expectations. I had other role models, some that were positive and others not so positive.

Picture living in a two-family home, one in a row of eight that had front steps that ended in a dirt landing. Across the street was Muschin's junk yard, filled with old and damaged cars. About two blocks away sat the Meiss junk yard, a very large operation spread out over several acres, and a haven for rodents, the homeless, and who knows what else. In the rear of our home there was a large garage that our landlord used to run his trucking business, and a block away sat the city dump. The smell of burning garbage wafted over the neighborhood, but we hardly noticed. It was just where we lived.

We kids had a ball living in Green Ridge. We used to find operating cars that had been junked, and the older kids drove the around the junk yard paths, having so many near collisions. And the dump was a treasure trove of goodies that we found as we hunted rats with our slingshots.

There were no swimming pools; heck, I had no idea what a swimming pool looked like! But we did have something better, and that was open mine swimming holes, or strip mines that filled up with water over time. That is where I learned to swim—to swim for my life—as we younger kids floated in tire inner tubes while the older guys cannonballed us from up on the stripping banks.

I can remember more than once being knocked silly and gasping for air, my arms flailing in the water until someone pulled me out. Picture this: There was no shore, just a steep drop-off, with nowhere to step out onto dry land. There were a couple of rocks that served as stepping stones, but you had to know where they were. When I was close to drowning, it was nothing but a stroke of luck that helped me make it to dry land.

Then one day someone told my mom about my swimming exploits, and she showed up as we frolicked in the water. What I vividly remember was walking home, bare (we never used bathing suits) with mom crying and hitting my backside with a switch she picked up along the way. It hit me then how I had frightened her, and how stupid I was to jeopardize my life for a few moments of fun.

So the fear of swimming in stripping holes stayed with me for a while. But boredom set in, and I found another challenge: going into abandoned coal mines. These were deep, anthracite coal mines. Can you imagine climbing down steep ladders and walking through blackness, through shafts that were dug by the hands of the coal miners? Since both my grandfathers were deep-mine coal miners, I could have been walking in their footsteps! These were adventurous times for an 8-to-10-year-old— times that took me close to death. But I wasn't afraid to take on a new experience, and boy-oh-boy, there were so many I enjoyed over the years.

Within sight of our front porch was a rail line that was used by steam-powered engines. I can still see the engines spewing billows of white steam, struggling to pull open hopper cars to the coal breakers. The breakers processed the large chunks of coal into several sizes that were sold to commercial and residential customers. No other fuels were used to heat homes and businesses and provide energy from the power plants.

I'm telling you this to set the stage for my next adventure. I used to take my wagon through the woods and the strip mines to the rail line. I'd position myself near an uphill grade where the train slowed down, and I'd climb up on one of the moving cars. While I was up there, I'd throw pieces of coal to the ground below, and then I'd jump off before the engineer saw what I was doing. I was caught a few times, but it was nothing more than the engineer screaming his head off, while I and the other kids I was with jumped to the ground laughing our heads off, knowing full well there was no action he could take against us.

Once on the side of the tracks, I'd load my wagon with the coal and pull it home. After unloading it in the backyard, I'd break the large pieces down to the size we used in the kitchen stove. You see, we didn't have central heat, only a big old kitchen stove that served to cook the food and heat the house. So there I was, doing what I could to help out, but never, ever telling my mom or grandparents where I got the coal.

When I was 10 years old we moved to Hazleton. This was like moving from an old, familiar neighborhood into the city, and I hated it. I loved where I came from and having fist fights with the Smontana and Voyda boys. If you fought the guy who was your age and won, then you had to fight his older brother ... and it went on until I got my head beat in and I cried "uncle. " That was what I knew, the culture that I grew up in. Moving to a neighborhood that was completely boring and without challenges made me one unhappy camper.

As I went through junior and senior high, I was an okay student, but I did get A-plus marks in fun. I had a ball and really enjoyed my classmates, teachers, and the entire experience. I learned how to get along with people and to be viewed, by some, as a leader. But as I reflect on my high school years, oh how I wish I had understood the value of education for everyone, regardless of what business or cultural interests they would eventually pursue. There is always a certain respect associated with the level of education that an individual attained. As I got older, I found myself gravitating to intelligent people, learning from them and trying to grow personally and professionally.

I share these stories with you because these were my formative years, and the experiences I had as a child and a teenager went a long way toward building my personality. I was tough yet caring, wild but with an inner fear about the consequences of my actions. Looking back, I wish I had shown my parents and grandparents how much I loved them. I also wish I had spent more time with my sisters, Janet, Nancy, and Dolores.

What I haven't shared yet are the reasons for the self-doubt and lack of self-confidence that have fueled my passion for working as a team member and helping people to be the best that they can be, using their inborn talents and positive personality. You see, I truly believe that we are all born with a positive outlook on life, and what leads us down the path of negativity are the people who can influence our lives.

In my case, I had uncles and several others whose constant comments about how I was a "bad boy" and wouldn't amount to anything still ring in my ears today. I don't remember anyone except my mom and her parents coming to my defense, giving me hugs and telling me I was going to be the president of the U.S.A.! And I can vividly remember my mom telling me that I was a very good boy. Talk about a high ... but it didn't overcome the emotional damage that was done. When I had an accident while using my chemistry set, spilling burning alcohol and ending up with second-degree burns, my uncle screamed at me for the trouble I was causing the family. A few years later, when I was shot in the leg during a hunting trip, all hell broke loose: "There's Joey, in trouble again, always causing trouble."

So I went through my formative years with the feeling that I was a troublemaker and a family problem. Yet that negative feeling did have a positive impact: It led to a commitment to make my family proud. I vowed to be a model husband and father, and a successful businessperson. I didn't climb the highest hill and proclaim my plans to the world, but instead went about it through hard work, commitment, and a desire to please.

Lessons From the Wider World

I just didn't see myself going on to college, as I knew my parents couldn't afford four years of higher learning, plus I didn't have a lot of self-confidence. So, as you can see, it was a bit of a conundrum: I was a hot-shot leader on one hand, and someone with low self-esteem on the other! After graduating from high school in 1958, I realized that I had to learn a trade, and that I had to go beyond a 12-year education. I found and enrolled in a transportation school in Minneapolis, Minn. The tuition and living expenses were a stretch for my dear mom, as her only source of income was from the salary my dad got from the Army.

So it was off to Minneapolis on a Greyhound bus, without friends, no place to stay, and a big lump in my stomach. My mom and my girlfriend, Regina, agonized over my departure and prospects for finding an apartment after arriving in a city that was absolutely huge when compared to Hazleton, and over 1,000 miles from home.

I stayed in a YMCA for a week, until the school found me a room to rent from a local family. I started classes and buckled down as never before, because I appreciated the sacrifices that my mom and sisters were making so I could go to school. I did very well, really applying myself and finding that it was relatively easy to be at the top of the class.

I also started working after school and on weekends. After school I baled paper in a paper recycling company, and on weekends I raked leaves at an apartment complex. That way I was able to earn spending money and ease the financial burden on my mom.

After a year I graduated. I turned down a few offers to work for the airlines in Minneapolis, as I wanted to get home. At this time I was

19 years old, and to say I was inexperienced in business is an understatement. Shortly after arriving back in Hazleton, I was hired by Dorr-Oliver, a manufacturer of filtration equipment, pumps, and other filtration products. The management team took a liking to me, and I moved along quickly. After 19 months I was put in charge of the second-shift shipping department. Imagine this—an inexperienced kid supervising 20 experienced, hard-nosed union workers! When I came on the scene I could see them chomping at the bit to take me apart.

It didn't work out that way, because I inherently knew the value of team play and how to collaborate. After a short time, my team was significantly outperforming the day shift, which had 50 percent more shipments. My team was kicking butt and they really enjoyed the experience. How did I do it? I treated people the way I wanted to be treated. I reveled in their performance and showered them with heartfelt praise. I told them I knew nothing about the skills they used in their jobs, and that I depended on them to help me help them.

Around that time, my dad suggested that I join the Pennsylvania National Guard; by doing so I would avoid the draft. After serving and retiring as a career noncommissioned officer, he was convinced that I would be better off joining the Guard. So I followed his advice and was soon off to boot camp. It was here that I met my next role model, Sgt. Dorsey. He was a huge drill instructor who was all over us—it seemed like 24/7. Sgt. Dorsey taught us discipline, orderly conduct, and team play, and that we had far more strength and endurance than we ever imagined. I'll never forget when our company competed in the divisional drill competition and came in second place. The disappointment that Sgt. Dorsey felt was written all over his face, and he told us that he had let us down.

Wow, was this an invaluable lesson learned—taking personal responsibility for your actions and, more importantly, that it's important to have a purpose in life. Sgt. Dorsey felt strongly about preparing us for what we might experience in both our military and civilian lives. He demonstrated his commitment and purpose in life every day.

From basic training I went immediately off to fourth months of Military Police training, which was uneventful. I returned home and rejoined Dorr-Oliver, and Regina and I married on January 21, 1961. But lo and behold, just a short time later, my National Guard unit was activated and sent to Ft. Polk, La.

So I was off to Louisiana, leaving behind my honey, who was expecting our first child in November. Our unit arrived in Fort Polk, an Army base that was mothballed after World War II. There were wild bulls, armadillos, snakes, and broken-down barracks. Talk about depressing! Unfortunately that was followed by an accident that landed me in the hospital for three months.

After being discharged I finally made it home in February 1962 and met Laure, my first baby girl. I immediately knew that I couldn't return to duty without my family, so after two weeks, off we went to Alexandria, La., where we lived until my unit was deactivated in August. We then returned to Hazleton, and I rejoined Dorr-Oliver.

But I was bored and knew that I had to get myself ready to move on. I enrolled in evening school at the University of Scranton, a fine Jesuit university. Shortly thereafter, I learned that International Salt Co. had an open position at its company headquarters in Clarks Summit, Pa.

I'll never forget driving up International Salt's private drive, coming to the top of the hill and looking at the ultramodern office building, with acres of grass, trees, landscaping, and a practice green. The juxtaposition of this view with the junked cars, open strip mines, and poverty I had grown up with blew me away! What the heck was a kid from Green Ridge doing here in this magnificent setting?

I signed in at the main desk, gazing up at the three-story-high ceiling and down at the ceramic tile floors. I had never been in a building like this before and was duly impressed. Shortly after arriving, I was whisked off to an interview room, where I completed some forms and was interviewed by the personnel manager. Then, with a flurry of movement, in came the director of the department that managed transportation and all field operations. I was hit with a barrage of questions and made to understand that this was one busy man who didn't have any time to waste on small talk. I worked into my response that I was a heck of a hard worker and dedicated to doing the best I could at any assignment. (I learned about hard work very early. I started working in my uncle's bakery when I was 10 and later at a bowling alley. In fact, throughout my entire career I was never out of work, not for a day!) I pitched him on my experience and plans to finish my degree, whether or not I got the job.

He surprised me by inviting me to lunch, across the street at the country club, accompanied by the director of manufacturing. Another great experience, but I quickly realized that I didn't know what spoon to use or where to put my napkin. The conversation was light and airy, with me mostly listening as the two big guys talked salt business.

Then it was back to the office where he grilled me on my goals and ambitions, and asked penetrating questions about my strengths and weaknesses. He needed to understand why I thought I should be considered, as I didn't have a business degree, whereas the position requirement clearly identified a degree as an absolute necessity. I remember saying that whether I was chosen or not, I was going to finish my degree. With that, he asked me to get up and walk around the room so he could get a good look at me, to see if my shoes were shined, and so forth. Yes, he was big on personal appearance.

Within a week, I was offered the position and given a couple of weeks to make a decision. My wife and I talked it over and decided to take the gamble; after all, it wasn't like I was going to lose anything if it didn't work out. Just to pass muster and be offered the position gave my ego a shot in the arm. I thought about my dad and Sgt. Dorsey, who had taught me about shining my shoes, wearing highly starched shirts, and having my "gig line" straight at all times. (Gig line, a military term, refers to having the fly, belt buckle, and shirt buttons perfectly aligned.)

I couldn't believe how fortune had reached down and touched me. I arrived at the office substantially earlier than the start time, stayed late in the afternoon, and took short lunch breaks. My manager was a longtime veteran of the company, well known and respected in the industry. He was great technically but far from a leader. If I didn't ask questions, we rarely spoke. So I worked closely with my department cohorts and learned about the Interstate Commerce Commission (ICC) and *Ex Parte* releases, all part of the regulated transportation infrastructure that existed at the time.

Given that the traffic department was small, the opportunities for promotion were limited. However, I was a quick learner and was soon recognized as a player, someone who added value to the management of both motor and rail transportation.

My job was a whirlwind of activity, and I was constantly being called upon to participate in various tasks, studies, and strategies. Over three years, I was called on for numerous assignments, including operations management for some 30 bulk salt facilities and salt warehouses, as well as motor and rail transportation. I was responsible for moving millions of pounds of salt from mines located near Detroit and Cleveland by ship across the Great Lakes, on barges from the Louisiana mine up the Mississippi, and by bulk ships from the Netherlands Antilles or Baja California. I either knew what I was doing or was able to spin a tale or two that captured the imagination of my peers and others in the company. The kid from Green Ridge was doing well at International Salt Company and in night school, where I carried a B-plus average.

And then I somehow found myself having cocktails at the country club, after work or over the weekend. Playing golf, followed by dinner and more cocktails and shooting billiards was part of the drill. My director hated to lose at golf or pool, and we stayed at it until he won or I just gave up.

By that time I enjoyed access to the company plane and other perks, which included being treated as the department head, as the director had a habit of taking long weekends, missing meetings, etc. On one hand, I was on a high, and on the other, the intensity of that busy, demanding life began to take its toll. Around that time, my dear mom came down with a rare and incurable form of cancer, requiring three major surgeries at Memorial Sloan-Kettering Hospital in New York City. (We had already lost our dad, to a heart attack, at 51.)

Mom passed away on April 22, 1971, at the age of 54. Her loss was devastating not just for me but also for my wife Regina, daughters Laure and Gina and sisters Janet, Nancy, and Dolores. To say that it was a trying time is an understatement. We just couldn't imagine life without the light of our lives. But somehow we persevered and plodded on with our memories.

But our trials that year weren't over. On August 21, Regina, Laure, Gina, and I were severely injured in a car accident. I had recently resigned from International Salt to enter the modular housing business. This would be my leap into the role of entrepreneur, something I had always felt was in my future. The job required a household move, and we were returning from dinner in my first new car, a very large, two-door Chrysler, talking about the moving company that would be at our home the next day and the last-minute packing we would have to complete when we got home.

To this day, I don't remember seeing the truck that came roaring at us as we drove down the two-lane country road. He hit us head on, crushing the front end and buckling the roof and the lid of the trunk. I have no memory of the next few days, either; I teetered on the brink of death, in a coma. I woke up some four days later in intensive care at Scranton General Hospital. In a daze, I looked to my right and saw a child whose head was wrapped in bandages

Moving On

The day I left Nabisco, November 28, 1998, I started with Americold, a supplier of cold storage and services, and OMI International. The CEOs of both companies agreed to let me split my time equally between them, because they felt they could make good use of my knowledge of the food industry on one hand and of supply chain management on the other.

OMI was owned by two individuals who had built the business, which provided retailers with very sophisticated software. The software covered everything from warehouse management and procurement to accounts payable and receivables. This was a great opportunity to learn about systems utilized by retailers and the positive impact the software could have on their balance sheet and profit-and-loss (P&L) statement.

Americold was owned by a leveraged-buyout company that was clueless about the cold storage business, but oh, were they flush with ideas. The controlling company's only concern was cash flow and paying down their debt. It was a fiasco, and I couldn't wait until my employment agreement ended.

OMI, however, was a totally different experience and a great opportunity to learn about the grocery industry from the perspective of the retailer. I had a great relationship with one of the owners, but not so much with the other. It was awkward at times, but that was outweighed by the fact that I had so much flexibility and so many opportunities to work with the trade, building my already extensive network. I attended every grocery trade event, including several conducted in Europe. One time I asked for permission to travel to Barcelona, Spain. The owner asked, "Do you think it's a good idea?" "Yes," I enthusiastically replied, and was shocked by his response: "If you think it's a good idea, why are you asking me for approval?"

OMI sold out to Retalix, an Israeli company that serves retailers' systems needs. During the transition I spent two weeks in Israel, with ample time for sightseeing and getting to know the culture and enhancing an already strong appreciation for the Jewish people. There were a number of long days and longer nights. Toward the end, I knew I didn't fit the Retalix culture and decided to go my separate way.

Within a month of the Israel trip, my OMI mentor met me at the Newark, N.J., airport to let me know I had been terminated. We laughed, shook hands, and parted company friends.

In 2005 I met with the board chair of VICS, the Voluntary Interindustry Commerce Solutions Association. VICS' objective was to help companies in the extended retail supply chain implement the organization's guidelines, best practices, and specifications, which would allow them to better anticipate and react to changes in consumer demand. By doing that they could improve their supply chain efficiency and effectiveness, sales, profits, and the use of fixed and working capital.

The chairman and I had known each other for a few years, as I had served as a member of the VICS board while I was with Nabisco. It was a short discussion, ending with an offer to join VICS as an executive, which I accepted without discussing salary. I was pleasantly surprised by the compensation that was included in my employment agreement! I worked at my normal pace; the VICS board approved of my performance, and within six months I was promoted to president and CEO.

Working for VICS was such a great opportunity to continue my retail education and gain a greater understanding of the importance of technical standards. I dealt with all the problems that are common to associations, but I also made a number of very important contributions, building guidelines for apparel, electronic data interchange (EDI); Collaborative Planning, Forecasting, and Replenishment (CPFR, a concept trademarked by VICS), and logistics.

The most important project to my mind was the development of the VICS Item-Level RFID (radio frequency identification) Initiative, or VILRI. A partnership with the University of Arkansas and its RFID Lab resulted in three pilots with major retailers, all of which had very positive results. That had a major impact on moving item-level RFID forward. (You can learn more about this in Chapter 7.)

In late 2012, VICS merged with GS1 US, a nonprofit organization that develops and promotes the use of standards for data used in supply chain management, like bar codes and global trade identification numbers (GTINs). It was a natural evolution, and I moved on knowing that VICS had created significant and lasting business value.

With that, I founded the Collaborative Energizer LLC, and at the same time decided to write this book. Collaborative Energizer LLC is a supply chain management and logistics consulting company. The company champions new technologies in item-level RFID that enable corporations to track and maintain inventory in real time. It also assists companies in understanding and developing collaborative business practices, change management skills, and the value of developing internal and external trusting relationships.

Confronting Life's Challenges

As I think back over the many places I've lived, the positions I've held, and the people I've known, I realize how valuable it has been to have the tenacity to work through the most difficult of times, and the ability to overcome and recover from adversity.

I could not have done it without the loving support of my wife Regina, who has played a critical role in every aspect of my life. The frequent household moves we made were tough on her, but she supported them. It was hard for the girls, too, as they were pulled from one school and had to start over at another so many times. That is something I would not do if I had the chance to do it all over again.

At the time, though, I felt I had no choice. You see, as I grew up, I believed that as an employee, you just didn't say no to management when you were asked to take a new position or accept a relocation. For example, in 1976 I was promoted by Standard Brands to Southwest regional manager, and we moved to Dallas, Texas. About a year later, we were moving back East; I'll never forget how devastated Laure and Gina were when I broke the news. It meant they would attend three schools in just two years, which was not fair! Oh, I should mention that I accepted the new position for the outstanding salary increase of $1,500.

The girls were not the only ones who were experiencing frequent changes in their lives. As mentioned earlier, over the next three years, I worked for three companies—as an inventory manager for a fabrication company, a sales rep for Lederle Laboratories, and another stint at Dorr-Oliver as traffic manager. We struggled to get back on our feet, with Regina carrying most of the emotional burden.

The period following the loss of my mother and the 1971 car accident was among the most trying of our lives. There have been two others

24

times as an adult when I nearly died—experiences that have made me realize how fragile life is, and how fortunate I am to have a loving, caring family. One happened in 1971 as we were being treated in the Scranton General Hospital after our auto accident. The doctors had decided that due to the severity of my injuries, they would focus their efforts on Regina, Laure, and Gina. Somehow word got to our family, and my Uncle Guy and Regina's brother George were brought to the emergency room. Guy noticed that I had been left on a gurney off to the side, and he demanded that the doctors do whatever they could to save my life. As George told us later, Guy said, "He is a family man, a father!" Thanks to him, the doctors went to work and I got another chance at life. Gotta love Uncle Guy.

The other happened in Clearwater, Fla., in 1995. One night I passed out around 11 p.m. Regina heard me fall. She came running, found me, and shook me hard. She called 911, and soon we were on our way by ambulance to the local hospital. Doctors there couldn't find the problem and decided to release me. But Regina begged them to keep me for observation, so they put me in the telemetry ward.

During the night, my heart stopped again, setting off an alarm, which brought the medical team to the rescue. I remember a lot of people in white jackets, paddles in hand, shaking me. "Mr. Andraski, Mr. Andraski, wake up, wake up!" I did wake up and immediately felt sick to my stomach. The next morning, when Regina and Laure walked into my room, I felt well enough to joke with them a little. "Guess what happened last night?" I said. Laure immediately bolted to the nurse's station to find out what happened. Not long after my release, a well-known heart specialist at another hospital quickly diagnosed the problem and scheduled me for pacemaker surgery.

So if Regina had not protested the hospital's plan to discharge me, I might have had an episode during the night and silently passed away. So here was yet another time God reached down and saved my life.

I think it's important to share these gruesome stories to illustrate that it is possible to bounce back from adversity, by the grace of God, even in the toughest of times. You have to keep in mind that every circumstance is different, but if I can do it, then so can others.

In fact, I am hopeful that the personal story I've told in this chapter will be inspirational and stand as an example for what can be accomplished by taking lemons and making lemonade. Throughout your life there will be those who just don't like you, for whatever reason, legitimate or not. That is the political aspect of business, which has to be accepted for what it is. The important thing is to just do what you know in your heart is right.

Chapter 2: Times of Change and Turmoil

In this chapter, I'll provide an overview of the evolution of Standard Brands, Nabisco Brands, RJR Nabisco, and KKR Nabisco while explaining how disruptive it was for most of us who worked there. Nabisco and its various parent corporations were huge organizations, with multiple events and changes taking place simultaneously. So there isn't a simple time line that I can follow or a way to discuss developments so they're neatly aligned. But this history will give you some background for understanding the constantly changing environment that I and the logistics and supply chain organization had to function in. And as we'll see in later chapters, despite all that change and turmoil, our group managed to innovate and succeed on every level. I can also recommend that you read *Barbarians at the Gate: The Fall of RJR Nabisco*—a best-selling book and television movie by Bryan Burrough and John Helyar about the leveraged buyout of RJR Nabisco.)

So we'll start with Standard Brands.

Standard Brands

Standard Brands was formed in 1929 by J.P. Morgan with the merger of Fleischmann Co., Royal Baking Powder Co., E. W. Gillett, Widlar Food Products Co., and Chase & Sanborn Coffee Co. By 1940 it was the number two producer of packaged goods after General Foods. By

1955 the company was listed at 75 in the *Fortune* 500. Standard Brands made several acquisitions. It bought Planters in 1960 and the Curtiss Candy Company in 1964. The company merged with Nabisco in 1981 to form Nabisco Brands Inc.

As Standard Brands morphed into what was to eventually become Nabisco Brands (and what is today part of the Kraft and Mondelēz companies), my career track progressed to include leadership positions in supply chain, strategic planning, sales management, and customer marketing. As a result, I had the opportunity to observe the top executives who led Standard Brands, Nabisco Brands, and RJR Nabisco, and the vastly different personalities they exhibited. I think you will agree after reading their short vitae that they had very different backgrounds and business experience. Intuitively, that tells us that their priorities and approach to management were substantially different, and that the organization had to adapt to ongoing change as each CEO took the reins. I've provided my impression of several of them, but to be honest, these are my personal perceptions.

To be fair, most every one of these folks had limited bandwidth to provide strategic advice regarding product management and other key areas, as they were consumed with mergers, acquisitions, and other related challenges. They were left with little time to strategize or build the business for the future.

Weigl vs. Johnson

Henry Weigl had been promoted to chairman and CEO of Standard Brands in 1964. During his tenure, the company bought Clinton Corn Processing and Planters Peanut Co. Under Weigl, employees' wages were often frozen for years. There was an accounting manager in the Wilkes-Barre, Pa., regional office who had not had a wage increase in eight years. Weigl ruled with an iron fist and focused on increasing net profitability—and he did that successfully, with 20 annual profit increases since the 1950s. But the company was dying and key businesses tanking, including corn oil and wine. Yet Weigl couldn't see disaster looming and did nothing to build or acquire brands. He tightened the screws on spending in every way imaginable.

Just how tight was Henry Weigl? Peter Rogers, who was president of several Standard Brands divisions and Nabisco Brands business units, knew Henry well. I'm still in touch with Peter, and I'm indebted to him for contributing the following keen insights into what only he can relate, given his first-hand experience with Henry Weigl and his successor and nemesis, F. Ross Johnson. Ross was able to intelligently and with panache move into the senior management ranks of Standard Brands. But Weigl was determined to oust Ross, as he was just too flamboyant and a free spender of company money. I know you will find the following to be among the most candid comments you will ever read.

Henry Weigl

In the 1970s, we had rotary phones, and all phones in the New York office were locked after 5 p.m. When I was in New York (twice a month), I had to go to the street to make calls to my Chicago HQ to report on the outcome of our semi-monthly meetings, or to call customers, on a public phone at 58th and Madison. I still have one of those phone locks; they were inserted into any one of the finger holes, the key was turned, and then the rotary dial could not rotate.

All the time Henry was chairman, SBI never covered pregnancy under its medical insurance. Henry maintained that pregnancy was a self-inflicted injury, and therefore it should not be covered. As soon as he left, we added pregnancy at ZERO cost. The insurance carrier had NO companies that did not cover pregnancy, so it was included in the premium, even though it had never been used.

When Jim Marler visited the West Coast he always went for two weeks, as that was the policy when we traveled by train, and he never dared ask Henry to update the policy—he just followed it blindly. Initially, Jim was my "boss," and then I became his "boss"—possibly because I would fly to the West Coast when we were putting together a "revolutionary" sales and distribution organization, and fly back on the "redeye," spending only three days away from the office rather than two weeks. With Mr. Weigl, the old adage "It's easier to gain forgiveness than it is to get permission" worked, PROVIDING that the financial results improve.

To Henry, the advertising budget was always "discretionary" profit, and no money could be spent on advertising until the third quarter.

Only salesmen for Fleischmann Yeast had company-paid club memberships (Ross eventually had 19 company-paid memberships), and Henry always checked the left hand of sales people in the summer. If the left hand was whiter than the right hand, he would demand to know the person's handicap. If it was under 15, Henry would have them fired on the basis that a normal person needs to play at least three days a week

*in order to attain a handicap of less than 15, and as there are only two
weekend days in a week, he must be playing on company time.*

*On one occasion, when Henry gave me a lift home in his company
Chevy, he said, "Peter, I'm going to give you some serious advice.
When you get to the level where you are entitled to a chauffeur—as you
surely will—NEVER sit in the front with the driver." It took me several
days to realize that he was telling me not to be too friendly with
subordinates. Henry definitely had no time for "empowerment."
He was also very anti-Semitic.*

F. Ross Johnson held just about every top position there was at Standard
Brands. He was named president and COO in 1975, and chairman and
CEO in 1976. When Standard Brands and Nabisco merged in 1981 to
form Nabisco Brands, he became the president and COO, then vice-
chairman and CEO in 1984. When Nabisco Brands and R.J. Reynolds
Industries Inc. merged in 1985, he stayed on as president and COO,
and in 1987 he became CEO. All this time he held various positions
on the executive committee and the board of directors.

Ross was different than Weigl in many ways. His main objective was
to serve the investment community. He was a free spender, entertaining
celebrities from sports, industry, and politics. He believed that from
the moment an organization was created it began to decay. He found
Standard Brands to be so terribly outdated that he was determined to
make change happen.

As was reported and covered in *Barbarians at the Gate,* Ross lived the
good life on his company expense report, with limos, country clubs, and
first-class travel (gradually building the Nabisco Brands "air force" of
some 15 planes). Team meetings started at his favorite dinner haunts,
followed by "business discussions" that went into the early morning
hours. He not only enjoyed his lifestyle, he also provided limitless perks
to those who were lucky enough to be on his team! As he walked the
company through each merger and acquisition, he bestowed upon the
Nabisco and RJR leadership bonuses, salary increases, and perks piled
upon perks. These practices bought him loyalty and commitment.

When Ross was named chairman of the board, he made two decisions:
1) that Standard Brands would move from the bottom of the industry
salary index to the 75th percentile—a huge move that took several
years to achieve; and 2) that the company would pay associates the IRS
allowance for personal autos used on company business. This definitely
demonstrated that Ross cared about the people in the company.

30

He listened to advice from his senior management team, which included Peter Rogers, a person who thought "out of the box" and truly cared about doing what was right for the company and for the people who made it successful. Peter joined Standard Brands in Canada as president of the candy and chocolate manufacturer Walter M. Lowney. He later held a number of high-level positions at Standard Brands in the United States, including CEO of the Curtiss Candy Co., followed by his appointment as group executive in charge of all of Standard Brands' U.S. operations and global information technology (then called MIS). He left the company for a few years and returned after the merger with Nabisco. His subsequent positions with Nabisco Brands included president of Life Savers, chairman and CEO of the Nabisco Biscuit Co., president of Nabisco Brands USA, and president of International Nabisco Brands.

Although I was always several levels below Peter in the management ranks, I got to know him well. I found him to not only have a deep understanding of every aspect of the business but to also be accessible, friendly, and helpful. He always took the time to get to know as many people in the organization as possible, and not just superficially. He made every effort to give us the tools that allowed us to be the best that we could be. I've had the opportunity to get to know a significant number of senior leaders, and can candidly say that Peter serves as a role model for every senior executive. Ross was fortunate to have Peter on his team, and that Peter was willing to accept numerous and varied assignments to strengthen any area of the company that was not contributing to the success of the whole. Peter was a winner, and this was recognized by Ross, giving a clear message to company associates. This may not sound like much, but it demonstrated to the employees that he cared.

So, as you can imagine, Peter is well-placed to make the following comments on Ross and his era.

F. Ross Johnson
In the late 1960s, the board of directors began to worry that Henry Weigl had no succession plan; whenever a key manager was identified as "having potential," Henry fired him. Thus the board decided to hire a potential successor to run Canada: Earl McLaughlin, chairman of the Royal Bank of Canada, who was on the U.S. board and was chairman of the Canadian board. So it was hoped that he could run interference and block any actions by Henry. Ross Johnson also was hired. One of Ross's management theories is that it takes at least three key guys to run any business, and that no business is so big that it takes more than five

people. So he hired three key guys: Martin Emmett, a South African mining engineer who worked for Alcan; Vern Housez; and me. In fact, Ross and I "courted" for six months.

The Canadian business was a mini version of the U.S.—margarine, candy, Planters, liquor, yeast, plus pet foods (we had a 50-percent share of the canned dog and cat food business).

I was hired as executive vice president, ostensibly with responsibility for corporate groups such as human resources (HR), electronic data processing (EDP), engineering, distribution, research and development (R&D), and so forth, as the company was organized along functional lines with one sales force for all products, one VP of manufacturing, etc. On my first day, Ross told me to sit in his chair, as he was leaving for a month's vacation in Jamaica. He told me that I had full authority, but that he needed a plan of reorganization on his return.

I proposed that we eliminate the Nestlé-style functional structure and replace it with four, self-contained integrated divisions: Wines and Spirits; Grocery; Confectionery; and Bakery and Food Service. The Grocery Division was further divided into two units: Human Foods and Pet Foods.

When performance in the Canadian business improved (the pre-tax profits of my area tripled in two years), Henry realized that Ross was a threat and that he could not attack him, as the Canadian board had jurisdiction. So he hired a corporate "heavyweight"—Alan Proudfoot— to run Curtiss Candy Co. and presented him to the board as his choice as successor. Although SBI owned the majority of the shares of Curtiss, there were still some outside shareholders, and Curtiss operated on a 13 x four-week basis, while SBI operated on a 12 calendar-month basis, so Proudfoot was ostensibly CEO of a "freestanding" subsidiary company.

Very quickly the board realized that Henry was doing an end-run against Ross, so I received a phone call on a Tuesday in August 1973 from Frank D'Alessandro (Ross's boss) telling me to get on the next flight to Chicago, as Proudfoot was being terminated. I arrived at the Curtiss office on the Tuesday afternoon, but Proudfoot was not terminated until Friday, so I sat in a hotel out near O'Hare for three days.

Henry's next move was to hire a person to head up International as another possible successor, but the board quickly moved Martin Emmett into that job.

32

The next three years were "difficult," although I rose in Henry's esteem as we integrated Planters' non-grocery into Curtiss, bought Pearson Coffee Nips and Wayne Bun, and took on distribution for small sizes of Sun-Maid raisins while doubling market share for Baby Ruth and Butterfinger and growing pre-tax profits from $4.8 million to over $24 million in three years.

By 1976 we were all tired of Henry, so the great "Coup d'Etat" (Forbes Magazine, *1976) took place, and you know the rest.*

Eventually I got tired of Reuben Gutoff's emphasis on "form over substance" and "process over results," so I left to run America's largest fish company, which was in Chapter 11 bankruptcy. .... After three years, Ross called me saying that SBI was about to merge with Nabisco, and as I was the best operating guy and the best intuitive marketer he knew, he wanted me back on the team.

There was so much going on with the merger that most of the company's associates had little awareness of how all the changes would impact them. Selling off brands or companies was just something that had to be done. But the ongoing turmoil did reverberate throughout the company. Standard Brands' oath was a "commitment to use the fruits of the earth to provide a good quality of life for those we serve," and yet the curtains were drawing closed, and it was going to be up to Ross to make the changes necessary to save the company.

I didn't know Ross personally, but I did feel the dramatic impact of the decisions he made, in rapid fashion. In summary, he generously compensated his immediate team and also provided the resources to that team to provide industry-leading salaries, benefits, and bonuses to the rest of the company. Ross liked people and tried to do what was right for the company and for all the employees who made it successful. He really was a "people person," as evidenced by his choice of Peter Rogers as a member of his inner circle.

Frequent Changes at the Top

When Nabisco joined Standard Brands, and Nabisco Brands was born, **Robert M. Schaeberle** became chairman. Schaeberle led Nabisco through that merger and the merger with RJR. He retired as chairman and chief executive in 1986, after 40 years of service, just as the company moved toward one of the most contentious leveraged buyouts in history.

In 1988 F. Ross Johnson was trying to gain control of the entire company, and he began working with the investment firm Kohlberg Kravis Roberts. Ultimately, KKR's bid prevailed, and soon after KKR began selling off pieces of RJR Nabisco.

Louis V. Gerstner Jr. was the chairman and CEO of RJR Nabisco from 1989 to 1993. I had the opportunity to meet with him a number of times, to deliver presentations as part of the management team and to witness his interactions with associates who were at different levels and in different operations. I developed the impression that he was not very excited about or very comfortable in his role. This was especially true when the tobacco industry went into a tailspin as lawsuits were successfully filed and adjudicated in the plaintiffs' favor. The financial awards to the states were enormous, placing a huge amount of pressure on all aspects of RJR Nabisco.

In my experience, Gerstner related differently to people at all levels of the organization; he had an outgoing and friendly approach with employees at the clerical level, but the higher an individual was in the organization, the cooler and more distant Gerstner became. He left RJR Nabisco in 1993 and went on to become chairman and CEO of IBM, where he was credited with turning that company around.

H. John Greeniaus joined Standard Brands in 1977. He was named president and CEO of Nabisco in 1989 following KKR's buyout of the company and served in that position until 1993. He then became chairman and CEO until his retirement in 1997.

I knew John and found him to be knowledgeable about the various aspects of the business, and I thought he was a good role model as CEO. From my experience, he was very complimentary, having written me numerous congratulatory and thank-you notes for the logistics team's accomplishments or for awards I had received. In my opinion, he was the glue that kept the company together during several years of turmoil. He and Peter Rogers were the two key executives that I could understand and relate to during my time with the company.

In 1998 I attended John's retirement luncheon. I felt honored to be there to wish him the best that life had to offer. At the luncheon, John said in his Canadian accent, "Joe, I can't believe you are still here!" With that he broke into a hearty laugh. I responded by saying, "John, I'm only here because of you, but now that you are leaving, my career with the company will come to a rapid end." We all laughed. And in fact, it wasn't long after that I left with my severance package to start a new business life.

34

There were other CEOs and board chairmen during the RJR/KKR era, but I never met them so I can't offer any observations. They included:

- **Charles M. "Mike" Harper,** who was tapped as chairman and CEO of RJR Nabisco as he was preparing to retire from ConAgra Inc., where he was chairman. He stepped down as CEO in 1996.
- **J. Paul Sticht,** who had been a C-level executive at R.J. Reynolds since 1968, including stints as president, CEO, and chairman of the board. He was brought out of retirement for a few months in 1987 to serve as chairman of RJR Nabisco Inc., and then returned for a brief time in 1989 as acting chairman and CEO, after the acquisition of RJR Nabisco by KKR.
- **Charles E. Hugel** was chairman of the board of RJR Nabisco in 1988. I never met him.

The Impact of Organizational Change

While all of these machinations were taking place, there was a team of dedicated and committed associates who kept the parts of these great machines churning together, getting through the toughest of times with hard work and perseverance. No doubt there was tension between Standard Brands and Nabisco. The differences between direct store delivery used by Nabisco and the conventional grocery delivery/ sales system used by Standard Brands kept the companies at bay. Nevertheless, many benefits were realized by bringing the companies together (for example, in procurement).

With so many changes in corporate ownership and leadership, it should come as no surprise that organizational changes were made at all levels. The specific impacts of some of those changes on the logistics and supply chain organizations will be discussed in later chapters, but the following story will give you an idea of the kinds of disruption we experienced.

Many of the changes were made for political reasons—in other words, to appease certain executives. For example, in 1987, when the corporate headquarters of RJR Nabisco moved to Atlanta from Winston-Salem, N.C., there was a significant backlash from the community and its leaders. They recognized the negative financial impact Winston-Salem would endure as positions were moved to Atlanta and people lost their jobs. The leadership of RJR fell into disfavor, resulting in a decision later on to move the Planters LifeSavers division, with some 250 positions, to Winston-Salem.

Concurrently, a sales and logistics department was established within Planters LifeSavers, creating stress and tension for those who had to move to Winston-Salem to keep their positions. Then there were new job descriptions and performance rating criteria that RJR had set up with the move. RJR salaries were at a lower scale than those for Nabisco Brands personnel, which was to be expected given the office relocation. Nevertheless, Nabisco Brands associates with years of service had to take significant cuts in their salaries. When people requested exceptions, the RJR human resources department was quick to remind them that the sales revenue generated by the smallest RJR brand was equal to or greater than Planters LifeSavers' total sales. So the path of least resistance was the clear one to follow.

This was but one of the numerous organizational changes that took place over the course of time, made for reasons that the staff rarely understood. For example, there were the integration of packaged Del Monte products into the organization, the acquisition of a cookie/cracker business in New York, and the acquisition of small product lines from a variety of companies. Everyone was tasked with supporting any senior executive team decisions and to ensure a successful implementation.

Every organizational change had financial, personal, and other consequences that had to be dealt with on the run. The management team had to deal with the changes with a positive, "can do" attitude. The information technology (IT) team was under such terrific pressure to make the necessary system changes that at times they had to put value-add improvements on the back burner. The staff felt like full-time firefighters, constantly dealing with HR, operational, and inter-organizational challenges that resulted from each of those organizational changes. There is little doubt that there was a significant financial penalty paid, over and over again. However, we adapted, improvised, and overcame (to use a U.S. military battle cry), so as not to lose the credibility that we had earned with the executive management team.

An important consideration during times of change is the personal feelings that we have: We like, dislike, or are neutral about the people we work with or those with whom we have some involvement. Do we dislike certain people because they are the "loudmouths" in the group, outspoken and constantly expressing their ideas? Or because of the organization they came from or were with at a particular point in time?

36

I don't pretend to be a psychologist, but I have seen one example after another where a decision was made to move, promote, or terminate a person based on emotion rather than on fact. I believe that was what happened to me in one case, but I couldn't get HR to give me an answer to any of my questions. Having received a number of complimentary notes from senior management as my November 1998 departure from Nabisco was in motion, I can only conclude that it was all because there was someone who didn't like me.

Of course, all of us on the management team had the opportunity to leave and seek a position with another company, but for the most part, we stayed with the ship. We were loyal to the senior executive management team.

There's no textbook that can lay out the right decision(s) that must be made when it comes to dealing with the political context for organizational changes. It's a matter of reaching back to your prior knowledge and experience, and using that in combination with a gut feeling to come up with the best way to move forward. The best advice is to keep a level head in the face of adversity or opportunity, and to remain calm and positive.

Chapter 3: Nabisco's Integrated Logistics Organization

The organization I worked for started as Standard Brands, Distribution Division, and later merged with Nabisco Inc. This chapter will give you an idea of how we developed Nabisco's Integrated Logistics organization, and who was involved. I can't say enough about the people I worked with during those years. That's when we bonded as a team and, more importantly, as friends. Our friendships continue today, some 35 years later. We have a Nabisco Alumni group, whose members communicate regularly and occasionally get together for regional dinners. The dinners always include stories of days gone by, of fun times and camaraderie. Everyone is of the opinion that working at Nabisco back then was one of the best experiences in their careers. (You can read a number of my teammates' reminiscences of those days in the Appendix.)

We'll start with a general overview, take a brief detour to pay tribute to two of the memorable personalities I had the pleasure of working with, and then look at those challenging times through the lens of my personal experience.

Overcoming Challenges One by One

The Nabisco Integrated Logistics organization evolved over a period of some 25 years, beginning with the consolidation of several major products under the Standard Brands banner. This was years prior to the food industry's emphasis on collaborative customer service, metrics, sustainability, risk management, and global supply chain management. In the early years Standard Brands' distribution management team consisted of a vice president of distribution, several director positions, and five regional customer service managers.

The customer service regions were basically responsible for the daily tasks of order entry, shipping, receiving, and, of course, customer service. Planning was the responsibility of corporate, with logistics systems support being rudimentary at best. Accessing timely and accurate information was an ongoing challenge.

Finished-goods inventory was managed by the National Inventory Control System (NICS), a homegrown system that had been built at Standard Brands through the collaboration of the corporate inventory manager and an information technology specialist. This system provided inventory guidelines, parameters, targeted weeks on hand, reorder points and guidelines, amount of safety stock for each stock-keeping unit (SKU), and the use of sales forecasts. NICS was clearly at the leading edge of inventory management practices in the food industry at that point in time.

The total customer offering was a hodgepodge of products that were scattered across all the aisles in a grocery store, and which represented the primary source of sales. There were a daunting number of customers across all the food sales channels, each with its own sales representation. Included were dry, frozen, refrigerated, and food service and industrial products.

With such a broad array of customer service requirements and sales contacts, it was a challenge to manage day-to-day responsibilities. Developing a cadre of customer service specialists, by customer vertical and product group, was not easy. The primary focus of each department head—sales, marketing, manufacturing, and finance—was narrowly defined by individual metrics. Consequently there wasn't much in terms of team play or internal collaboration. Typically the distribution team was at the bottom of the totem pole of company politics. So if a customer service problem surfaced, the finger of responsibility usually was directed at distribution. This was prior to the introduction and use of new technologies such as distribution resource planning (DRP) that provided mission-critical information.

In the late '70s there was an emphasis at Standard Brands on improving the logistics system. This initiative started with a task force made up of representatives from distribution and information services (IS) and was sponsored by the corporate VP of finance. It was a true collaborative effort between the two departments; the individuals who were assigned to work on the project were well experienced in their specialties, and they were committed to developing cross-functional expertise. The project started with order management and led into inventory management, both directly focused on regional customer service. This was prior to the advent of formal collaborative programs, but it certainly had all the elements of a collaborative effort, and it proved to be highly successful.

We had plenty of challenges to address in improving service as defined by sales and our customer base. An important issue was that customers had their own methods of measuring the quality of a vendor's service, which were different than the metrics we used at Standard Brands to measure the quality of the service we provided to them. For example, a product substitution was considered a cancellation by the customer, and any order that was delivered after the customer-requested delivery date was considered a service failure, even if the customer didn't provide a delivery appointment. Consequently, the reported customer service metrics would appear to miss Standard Brands' case-fill and on-time delivery goals.

I took action to ensure that we reported service based on the *customer's* service score card. As we moved forward, service discrepancies—the difference between what we were reporting vs. the customer's metrics— aligned. This resulted in a revamping of distribution's metrics so that they were very stringent and aligned with those of our customers. In fact, a survey done around that time by Cleveland Consulting found that we had far more stringent service requirements than the other suppliers in the grocery vertical.

Technology Brings Improvements

While this progress was being made there was plenty of information that resided in our system that we couldn't get at without Information Services (IS) writing programs and cranking the mainframe for what seemed like days on end.

Back then the "system" was essentially a black box. We knew it had information, but did it have the information we needed? Access to necessary information required a request for service, which was placed in the IS queue, and then program modifications had to be completed. It could take several weeks to receive a response.

And then along came the "relational data base." Information could be accessed in hours and sometimes minutes! With very high processing speeds, large volumes of information were loaded into a distribution database with daily and weekly frequency. With this technology we were able to complete distribution studies in a short period of time and be confident of the conclusions we reached, because we had reliable, verifiable, and timely information.

Next came the personal computer. Our team quickly developed the necessary user skills, which we learned either while we were with the company or at a university. The "black box" version of information systems all but disappeared. Distribution was encouraged to be a partner in the use of the system and the development of new applications. In this user-friendly environment of computers, non-IS personnel who had an understanding of computers were invited to help develop applications that improved operations.

Building the organization was happening concurrently with developing a state-of-the-art supply chain management system, starting with order entry, inventory, transportation, customer service, and related support systems. We completely understood that regardless of the talent that we brought into the company, without the right technology we could not be successful. We were fortunate to have Demi Lappas and Joe Wisdo of Information Services working with us to develop the technology for our state-of-the-art supply chain management system. It was truly a team effort between IS and Integrated Logistics. That effort had measurable results that were clearly understood by senior management. Consequently, we received approval for the development of a sales forecasting system even though at that time we were deep into the Kohlberg Kravis Roberts & Co. (KKR) acquisition, when cash was king and money was hard to find.

Future chapters will provide more specific information on the programs that achieved dramatic results in managing transportation from both a cost and service perspective. But for now suffice it to say that this was critical, as transportation was approximately 75 percent of our total logistics costs. Motor carriers were networked into our system, and they were able to make customer appointments as well as schedule labor and equipment. Helping our carriers to be effective and efficient emphasized our commitment to working in a collaborative manner. We took the same approach with our public and private distribution centers and realized outstanding results.

We also built out a distribution resource planning (DRP) system that was purchased from Manugistics. It was purchased and integrated into our IL operating system and operative in just nine months. According to Manugistics, most other companies took years to make this happen, but our team was once again performing in an outstanding manner. We provided the highest levels of customer service with budgeted inventory levels, and we followed up with a material resource planning (MRP) system.

At this point we were ready for sales and operations planning (S&OP), led by Rick Blasgen, currently CEO of the Council of Supply Chain Management Professionals (CSCMP). When senior management was involved and committed, we witnessed the solid development of a company business plan. However, that wasn't always the case, and it was a very important experience to put in our quiver of knowledge.

There is little doubt that technology led the march toward innovation and unbridled progress in meeting or exceeding customer requirements, while concurrently allowing us to effectively manage administrative and logistics operating expenses.

This leads us to teamwork and "zero defects," both important concepts for our group.

We defined a true team player as one who can make the group or another individual look good without seeking credit for him/herself. This mindset was emphasized throughout our network of team players, within both the company and our service providers.

We defined zero defects as an ongoing process of continuous improvement that builds on prior achievements. One way we demonstrated the value and importance of zero defects was when we determined that processing a customer return cost eight times the original processing and cost of shipping.

There were so many other building blocks that we put in place to continuously improve our ability to exceed the expectation of our customers and our executive management team. It was very rewarding to witness the team rally around such key principles as:

- Constantly conveying the competent image provided by an orderly appearance and method of doing business, in both administration and operations
- Having concern for the morale of all team players, and ensuring open and honest communication, with no problem being too insignificant to be addressed
- Being clear about expectations, as team members can't perform if they don't understand what is expected of them
- Emphasizing the importance of education, including team management's responsibility to define requirements and structure an information system to measure performance to expectations
- Providing consistent and fact-based team feedback

The point to be embraced is that this was a step process, building an organization from the bottom up that would be capable of meeting and/or exceeding the company's goals and objectives. We measured sales dollars per associate; in other words, the greater the sales per Sales and Integrated Logistics (S&IL) associate the more effective we were perceived to be. But it had to start with a benchmark (i.e., sales per associate), which led to budgeted sale/associate year-over-year.

Management could therefore easily understand the productivity gains that were being made. Here's the message: Report metrics to senior management in terms they understand! They will have little interest in the cost per hundredweight for transportation or warehousing, but they will start paying attention when it's related to customer service, order fill, case fill, and favorable customer ratings.

At the same time, innovative management took place at all levels in the organization. Team players were encouraged to take responsibility and to assume a thought leadership role, without constant and suffocating oversight.

The results were extraordinary, as evidenced by the numerous teammates who have gone on to very successful careers, giving credit to their experience with Nabisco Integrated Logistics as the foundation for their success. And that's not all—industry surveys over the years have ranked the organization in the top three for food manufacturers' supply chain capabilities and service. And so the die was cast for the progress that is covered in the succeeding chapters.

Some Special Members of Our Team

There were many unique individuals who made outstanding contributions to the success of the distribution and logistics organizations at Standard Brands and Nabisco. I could write an entire book just about the amazing team members I've worked with over the years. Some of them are mentioned in various places in this book, and others are not specifically mentioned, but all of them played an important role in the success of their teams and of their companies as a whole. Although I don't have the space to give everyone as much "ink" as they deserve, I would like to call out two people who had a great influence on the Integrated Logistics team and on me personally. As you'll see, they were "part of the family" in more ways than one.

Joe Wisdo

Joe Wisdo joined Standard Brands shortly after graduating from Penn State University with a BS in Logistics in 1973. He was one of the very first Penn State graduates to be hired by the distribution department. He studied under Prof. John Coyle, who headed up the logistics program and always remembered Joe as one of his outstanding students.

Joe spent 25 years with Standard Brands and Nabisco. Over the years, he held many positions within the supply chain organization, including traffic manager, distribution center manager, manager of distribution systems, and director of inventory operations, among others. It was this broad experience along with his magnetic personality and collaborative mindset that positioned Joe well for his last position. Demi Lappas, the VP of information technology, became aware of Joe's talent when they worked together on several projects when Joe was the director of inventory operations. They formed a strong bond, working very well together, and Demi offered Joe a position as the senior director of IT.

Joe accepted, and in that position he directed a team of 50-plus programmers who worked on information systems that focused on sales, supply chain, and electronic commerce processes. His efforts improved customer service and helped to integrate various businesses within and outside of Nabisco's order-to-cash system.

Joe quickly bonded with his new team. Because of his background, he understood the importance of engaging his user "clients." He built operating systems with specific input from users, incorporating their feedback into the features and functions of each business requirement. He was a very effective team builder who easily worked across organizational boundaries.

44

The contribution Joe made to the success of Integrated Logistics cannot be adequately expressed. He was instrumental in two of the important IT achievements discussed earlier in this chapter: implementing the Manugistics distribution resource planning (DRP) system in just one year, and convincing the company to approve $25 million for a new sales forecasting system. The CEO at the time, John Greeniaus, approved this request based on the fact that we always delivered on our commitments. And once again Joe came through! That system eventually was sold to a technology provider for a tidy sum.

We could always count on Joe to deliver, regardless of the circumstances, as trying as they might have been. He will always be remembered for his deep, roaring laugh and outgoing personality. There is no doubt that we could not have been as successful as we were without Joe's mission-critical contribution.

Joe suddenly passed on February 14, 2013. He will be so sorely missed by his wife Dolores and his children, Cole and Jocelyn. I will also miss Joe, who was as close to me as a brother—in fact, he was my brother-in-law. I was always so proud of him and will forever keep him in my prayers.

Gabe Panaccio

Sometimes when I think about days gone by, some events seem like they occurred just yesterday while others feel like they happened a century ago. In the case of Gabe Panaccio, it feels like yesterday that we worked together, even though some 30 years have passed. You see, I still consider Gabe—my uncle, and someone I knew for most of my life—to be one of my role models.

Gabe was a salesman for a transportation company in the Northeast. He really knew his customers and all aspects of their business as it pertained to logistics. Constantly the top producer in the company, he was very much valued for his positive attitude and drive for perfection by his customers and his management team.

He served in WWII, and his hands suffered frostbite when he served on the front lines during the Battle of the Bulge. He had been on medication since that time, and some of his medical symptoms were attributed to severe frostbite. But there was something else going on, and we noticed that his light limp was gradually getting more pronounced. Eventually he had to retire from the company, as he could no longer gat around much. It wasn't long after that the company declared bankruptcy, which had a serious impact on Gabe's financial plans for his retirement, yet his attitude was always upbeat.

About that time I was working for Standard Brands, which was in the process of being acquired by Nabisco, with responsibility for logistics operations. As with all acquisitions, there were areas that were not managed well. We soon had a crisis on our hands: transportation loss and damage claims receivables had reached unseen heights, amounting to millions of dollars.

My feet were put to the fire, and I had to come up with a quick but sustainable solution. I reached out to Gabe, who at that point was housebound. I asked if he would be willing to take on claims receivables within the confines of his home. He agreed, and with that we set him up with an office and trained him on the claims and accounts receivables system.

I committed to my leader that the balance of claims receivables would be substantially reduced over a six-month period. I couldn't be much more specific, as I didn't know how much Gabe would be able to accomplish.

Gabe jumped in with all the excitement and enthusiasm of someone just starting his career. He quickly reached out to the carriers and established lines of communication, on as much a personal as a business level. His knowledge of the transportation industry was a personal asset. He understood the problems carriers dealt with when it came to loss and damage claims and the resources they had to commit in order to manage claims.

We saw almost immediate results! Loss and damage claims declined month after month. In discussions with plants, distribution centers, carriers, and members of our claims staff, we learned that Gabe was actually educating all of them. He quickly developed a strong relationship with the carriers, which translated to an atmosphere of trust among all the players.

Gabe's positive attitude and his holistic understanding of the challenges faced by all parties was infectious. His clarion call was "we work together." And by working together, our claims organization exceeded the stretch goals we had established. Gabe and his beautiful wife Jeannie were members of the Nabisco team for over 20 years. Long after their retirement, his admirers continued to stay in touch with them, which was a real testament to the role models they were to so many.

What makes this story more poignant is that Gabe suffered from multiple sclerosis, yet he continued working. He had fewer and fewer good days as his mobility continued to decline, but no one knew. He never complained, and when asked about his health he would always robustly respond, "I'm doing fine, how are you?" He didn't meet his extensive fan club until we honored him at a luncheon at the Philadelphia Airport. It was attended by his Nabisco colleagues as well as by carriers from across the country. Everyone in attendance was in awe of this giant of a man and his Jeanne. Yes, "we work together" was the silent chant that we repeated over and over. The accolades he received brought tears to the eyes of everyone who was there.

Gabe was a fighter who had to endure so many health issues, yet his attitude remained positive and upbeat. The debilitating consequence of MS had kept him homebound for many years, yet he inspired so many of us.

I think of how many challenges we all face in business and how much more successful we would be if "we all work together" as Gabe urged us to do. Uncle Gabe passed in December 2012, fighting for life to his last breath. The last time I saw him at the hospital, he could barely speak, so he whispered in my ear, "I love you." Uncle Gabe, we will always remember you.

A Rough Road Through Merger Territory

I joined Standard Brands in 1974, not really knowing what to expect, save for the fact that it was a large company with a number of easily recognized brands, including Planters, Royal desserts, Milk Bone pet snacks, Blue Bonnet margarine, and Fleischmann Yeast, among others. My first position was that of eastern regional traffic manager, with responsibilities for transportation for several public distribution centers and manufacturing facilities.

My first eye opener was the fact that I was traffic manager in name only, as each shipping point operated autonomously, utilizing a routing guide that was provided by the corporate traffic department. One of my main charges was to minimize the loss of pallets used to move product from plants to distribution centers and from distribution centers to customers. I had no leverage whatsoever over the carriers, as their bread was buttered by corporate.

Shortly after I arrived on the scene, the gentleman who hired me resigned. That was part of the plan going in, but no one bothered to clue me in on why he was leaving and who was replacing him. Much to my pleasant surprise, my new manager, Jim Nardi, was a stand-up guy who had his feet firmly planted in solid business practices and had a strong an understanding of the division between field and corporate responsibilities.

He was a Penn State grad, one of the first to go through the logistics program there and an individual who really had his act together. One of his first attempts to develop a sound working relationship with corporate was to call a meeting in Wilkes-Barre with the intention of aligning roles and responsibilities. This first meeting was a disaster, as corporate pushed back on each and every suggestion he made about who was going to do what in order to provide acceptable levels of customer service at reasonable operating costs.

So on a scale of 1 to 5, with 1 being failure, we ended up at a minus 4. The organization was buzzing about the turmoil being created by these two newcomers in Wilkes-Barre. How dare they roil up corporate! An ombudsman was sent to help iron out the issues and find neutral ground for compromise. That effort didn't work out, as this person had no responsibility other than that he worked for the VP of distribution.

Shortly thereafter Jim resigned to take a position with a Midwestern retailer. I was really sorry to see him leave, as we had developed a strong working relationship. He was replaced by Richard Price, someone I hardly got to know before I was promoted to southwest regional manager, which required a move to Dallas. I would be working for John Kenney, whose office was in Chicago.

So here I was, with limited company experience, in a regional manager's position. It wasn't very long before it became apparent that the region was really run by the sales team, and that they called the shots. The public distribution center marched to its own drummer and didn't recognize the regional manager, me, as the person they had to satisfy. We dealt with a host of service problems on a daily basis. My days in the office were long and getting longer as the days went by. I tried to spend as much time as possible at the public distribution center, the Planters manufacturing facility, the yeast plant, and with the regional sales managers.

As I delved into the regional office functions, I found so many operational and administrative disconnects that I didn't know where to start. Fortunately Bruce Montgomery, Donna Smith, Doyle Hall, and Dennis Tenery stepped up in each of their respective areas of responsibility and we began to make some real progress.

I recall hearing from John Kenney, my immediate manager, that he was moving on to another company and that some other changes were in the works. Wow, that meant that I would be working with four managers in a little over two years. I wasn't getting a warm and fuzzy feeling about my new company after a relatively short period of time. I wasn't sure how much support I had at corporate, if any at all.

Then Jim Varrato came on the scene as the VP of distribution, and I reported to him. After a few weeks in the position, he journeyed to Dallas and spent several days with me and our team. Jim was a real down-to-earth guy who had a keen understanding of both corporate life and the challenges of operating in the field. We spent time with each of the sales managers and visited each of the plants and distribution centers. Jim was very clear in regard to what he saw as the breakdown in responsibilities, and how he expected that we would all cooperate in exceeding customer service expectations on one hand and minimizing operating costs on the other. I really felt good as Jim and I said goodbye at the Dallas-Ft. Worth airport and I looked forward to a new start.

But it didn't work out that way. Almost immediately I was summoned by each of the plant managers, who adamantly expressed their displeasure with Jim. Where he did he get off thinking he could dictate anything to them, was their message. Only the public distribution center manager maintained a positive attitude toward our working relationship. However, he wanted to make sure that if I made any changes that would impact his operation's bottom line, those costs would be immediately passed on to Standard Brands.

Not long afterward, I was called to New York City and offered the position of northeastern area manager. I was ordered to find a replacement for myself in Dallas and concurrently make plans to move to Wilkes-Barre, the office at which I had started. It wasn't long after my family and I moved to the Northeast that Jim Varrato resigned and was replaced by Richard Price, who in the meantime had advanced to VP of distribution. (Later, my office was moved to corporate at Madison Avenue in New York City; we moved to Morristown, N.J., after the Standard Brands–Nabisco merger.)

Let me try to scope some of what was happening during these many changes. In addition to trying to learn as much as I could about the company customer base, sales, marketing, etc., I was also attempting to understand the operating systems that we used, or tried to use based on individual operating knowledge and experience. There wasn't much consistency between the regional accounting offices and sales practices. I couldn't help but be amazed at how a company could be as successful as it had been, considering the operating systems we didn't have through the end of the 1970s. As it turned out, I wasn't the only person feeling the need to develop a strong functional distribution system, as the decision was made to embark upon the development of a new system. We were so very fortunate to have Tom Gaughan, the VP of information systems, and his team of Bob Lyons and Al Goodrich assigned to work with us to write the functional specifications.

It's hard to put into context the many things that were taking place at the same time, including the acquisition of LifeSavers in 1980 and the challenges that brought to bear. I have to remind myself that at that point we had yet to bring together the Nabisco and Standard Brands businesses; the Food Service division was in a constant state of flux as the Nabisco folks did all they could to stay independent of the ongoing integration efforts.

Change—constant, unyielding change—was often driven by culture vs. what was right for the business. One nail that was driven into my heart was the change in my reporting relationship after I had been named as the operations director, with five regional customer service center managers working for me. Since we had known each other a few years and a couple of them were my protégés, it made my job that much easier.

My world became a lot more stressful when I learned at a company dinner that my reporting relationship would be changing immediately. I was to report to an inexperienced but highly political Nabisco person, with no explanation whatsoever. There was no rationale other than what I had conjured up, which was that this was a step toward integrating Standard Brands with Nabisco.

The first thing that happened was that my new manager immediately challenged one of my expense reports. I had used the company cell phone (yep, we had cell phones in 1981) to call my daughter, who had just started college, to make sure she was doing okay. I was called on the carpet and had to write a check reimbursing the company for $25. I was embarrassed and intensely angry.

50

That was just the first of a number of challenges this manager made on operating expenses, organizational changes, perceived customer service failures, and physical inventory differences. There wasn't anything I had done or that I was doing that met with his approval.

Then came the *coup de grace,* when I was sent to an eight-week Columbia University Executive Program. During that time I was forbidden to speak with anyone back at the company.

But I came to enjoy the program, which featured presentations by noted executives such as Jack Welch. There were 65 classmates from all around the globe. We bonded and enjoyed each other's company. Much to the dismay of my "superior," I was named class president, which was quite an honor given the executive positions held by my classmates. Oh, how I loved sharing my honor with the HR group and getting some positive press.

When I returned to the Morristown office, I quickly learned that my superior had made a number of phone calls to and visits with my direct reports. It was obvious to them that he was digging for any dirt he could find about my management style and whatever bones were buried in the tomb of my mistakes. They read his obvious desire to put me out to pasture, and they did everything they could to sing my praises, giving me high marks for my leadership and the gains the regions had made since the Standard Brands/Nabisco merger.

It didn't end there, as the tension between us never subsided, except when we were in the company of the executive team. Then it was all smiles and tales of success, which made my stomach churn.

At the very same time, the LifeSavers team was doing anything and everything to try to distance themselves from the features and functions of the system we were using to manage the business. LifeSavers insisted that their orders couldn't be combined with those for Planters or any other products for shipment to customers. They had their own homegrown practices that had far outlived their usefulness, but nevertheless, it was one complaint after another directed to the executive management team. Of course this provided fodder to my superior, but to no avail.

After a period of frustration on my part and that of the divisional president, there was a wise decision to have a noted consulting firm do a deep dive to determine whether LifeSavers' requirements were in fact unique. The consultants quickly pointed out that there were common customers, and that it was difficult to determine where the rub existed. It was soon concluded that there were minor differences that had to do with product allocation, but that they involved less than 5 percent of the business. So get on with managing the business and stop the bickering! Of course, being on the end that was responsible for customer service, I was constantly fielding complaints. Unfortunately, none of the investigatory work brought up concerns about LifeSavers sales and marketing failing to provide sales forecasting, business planning intelligence, or customer intelligence that was anywhere near adequate.

This leads me to step back a bit to write about the cultural environment that existed, not only with LifeSavers but with every one of the business units. The Nabisco Brands structure depended on business unit heads, who were responsible for marketing, market research, manufacturing, and co-packing. The matrix organizational structure had Sales and Integrated Logistics providing service to each of divisions, and this inevitably led to finger-pointing for any perceived problems. While I dealt with Integrated Logistics, there were sales executives who had to explain why sales objectives were not being met.

Of course, there was the corporate structure consisting of human resources, national sales, finance, etc. There were a number of senior executives who reported to John Greeniaus whom I never had the opportunity to meet; however, I determined that each had an opinion about some aspect of the logistics business and anything related to it. I usually became aware of this information during informal discussions with the individual I worked for at one point in time or another.

Getting to the point, in this "clandestine" organizational structure, a person's career could be impacted either positively or adversely.

For some reason, the corporate VP of human resources showed great favor toward a person who could have been considered a competitor to me. He never—not once—took the time to explain what the burr was that was under his saddle as it pertained to me, one Joe Andraski. Every one of my performance reviews indicated that I had exceeded plan and had delivered on the finances, which accounted for 50 percent of the rating. So if he had a problem with me, which had been suggested to me by several individuals, he never had the manhood to sit down and explain where he was coming from, ever.

At one point in time, this VP accepted a position with an Ohio company. Although it wasn't planned that way, after he left I was asked to take a position as national sales vice president, and I gladly accepted. However, after John Greeniaus announced his retirement, the former HR vice president decided to return to the company.

Here's the kicker. The first action he took upon his return was to pull me out of the sales job. No explanation, no rationale, nothing other than it was a dead deal. Now wasn't this a heartwarming decision on the part of someone who had not had more than a dozen words with me over 25 years? I remember telling John Greeniaus during his retirement luncheon that with him leaving, it wouldn't be long before I would follow. I said that in full earshot of the human resources VP.

This isn't sour grapes, as company politics exists in every organization. I do know that I can go eye-to-eye with anyone and everyone, and explain why I decided to do whatever. I only hope someday I get the chance to face him and call him a coward.

I had a knack for endearing myself to some of those to whom I reported, but I had a rocky relationship with others. I never could figure that out, as I was the same guy, being all that I could be, regardless of the circumstance. The only word I can come up with is "conundrum."

I think my record stands on its own, given the widespread acknowledgement that the business systems and processes we developed over some 25 years were so successful. I have had very positive recognition from leaders in academia, including those who are considered to be thought/concept leaders. I have also received numerous awards, as I've tried to give back to the industry as much as I received. What is most rewarding are the acknowledgements I've received from sales colleagues over the years, thanking me for helping to dramatically improve their understanding of the food business from both a process and a technology standpoint.

The point I want to leave you with is that everyone, at some point in his or her career, will find themselves at the short end of the stick and feel they are unfairly being taken advantage of by one or more individuals. With that in mind, if I had more confidence in myself, I would have taken a different career path. By that I mean that I would have sought out other opportunities, outside of Nabisco, and not allowed myself to be pushed from VP of national accounts to VP of strategic planning, and finally to VP of customer marketing without a commitment from the company to a career path that rewarded years of making positive contributions to the success of the company.

I'm explaining all of this because I'd like you to learn from my mistakes, which may or may not pertain to everyone. I never wanted to be part of the "in crowd," to live in the right neighborhood, to join the country club or fraternize with members of the executive suite. I'd rather have dinner with my wife and family instead of hobnobbing with those who could potentially have a positive impact on my career.

My focus was on getting the job done, and on improving the lot of the people in the organization I was responsible for, for the long term. Those who counted are still friends today.

I'm hopeful that you will find something in my experience that is beneficial to you. Most importantly, "to thine own self be true." No one other than yourself can suggest what that truth might be.

Chapter 4: Managing People and Organizations for Success

The Integrated Logistics organization learned the ingredients for success over some 25 years of never-ending turmoil and challenges. Some of this was not evident as we were involved in the day-to-day management of the business, but in retrospect it has become clear. So while we believe we added a significant amount of value and took the company out of the "dark ages" business-processwise, there were other success factors that have to be recognized. The following are some of the must-haves for staying power.

- *Quality and well-recognized brands.* Management will come and go, but quality brands will survive many poor business decisions.
- *A strong customer base.* Built over time with products that the consumer values, a strong customer base is an asset that is difficult to develop.
- *A strong and experienced sales force.* Building a close relationship with the customer is extremely valuable.
- *Leadership, at all levels.* This is an absolute essential. A leader who will take the reins and make positives out of potential negatives will inspire others, creating a cadre of leaders.
- *Change management.* It is critical to understand how to make change happen and recognizing when the need is pressing.
- *Ongoing communication.* Communication must take place consistently throughout the organization. Associates have to be constantly advised of the company's plans and what is expected of the team.

- *Respect.* Every associate has to be treated with respect. Everyone must understand that every position adds value and contributes to the overall success of the company.

Practically every business management book I have read has some reference to these recommendations, but the question is: to what extent are they followed? I can't recall any senior management meetings at Nabisco where these essential ingredients were discussed. Frankly, there were few presentations made by senior management that I could relate to. Did these individuals really understand what was taking place down in the "bowels" of the company?

With that in mind, in this chapter I'll discuss the challenges faced by Integrated Logistics and how I went about fighting the good fight and building one of the best organizations in the Nabisco stable. Certain factors—culture, politics, leadership, trust, and change management— influence the success of any organization, both positively and negatively. So along the way I'll also tell you about how those factors played out at Nabisco and affected our team. Then we'll finish up with some recommendations on building successful teams that are based on my experience.

Culture

I don't get it. And the "it" here is this: With all that was going on within Standard Brands and Nabisco Brands, RJR Nabisco, and KKR, plus the trade—you can't help but wonder how we made the progress that put us near the top of the brands/suppliers in the grocery and mass-merchant market categories. It can be mind-boggling thinking about managing just one of the events that took place over the life of these companies, and then imagine dealing with one event after another!

I'm convinced that the unique culture we built in Integrated Logistics played a big role in that success. I can honestly state that our culture was far different and more congenial than that of other organizations. The people and how we worked together, along with our work values and priorities, were the foundation of what we achieved. But it wasn't easy to get there.

The days were long, with constant distractions. Political maneuvering took place over and over again, creating an environment full of tension and uncertainty. For example, the division presidents were not always happy with being serviced by the Integrated Sales and Logistics organization—they argued that they didn't have control over two important functions that directly impacted their success. Yet it was made clear, time and time again, that these presidents didn't have the organization size nor did they have the bandwidth to fund individual groups. Then there was the corporate group and human resources (HR), which had to be included in many decisions, such as personnel and finance. Meanwhile, IT didn't have a good sense of what was needed to run the business, until Demi Lappas and Joe Wisdo took control and we bonded as a team to build the technology that led to the success we enjoyed.

The consequential changes that inevitably came about proved to be challenging and frustrating for the corporation, as each CEO had his own management style and game plan for success. In addition, those who were further down the organization chart constantly tried to understand each new strategy and anticipate what was of key importance to the top dog. Our Integrated Logistics team wasn't immune to feeling the tension brought on by the rumor mill and by uncertainty and change. And I was no exception. There were times when the knot in my gut felt like a large gnawing snail, which made it hard to concentrate and to stay focused on the business at hand. Fortunately the "snail" found someone else to terrorize, and I could go about my business.

Among the aces up our sleeve were the regional customer service centers. They brought us closer to the customers, distribution centers, transportation providers, and manufacturing facilities. At one time, total headcount for the centers and home office amounted to 110 individuals. The annual budget for transportation, warehousing, and administration was $120 million, which amounted to less than 5 percent of sales. No doubt we were one of the industry leaders when it came to cost to run the business and the high levels of service that were consistently provided.

We took great pride in our training and educational programs. We also felt strongly about our culture of excellent execution, and how that would set us apart from the other companies in the industry. The strong relationships we developed with academic thought leaders like Don Bowersox and M. Bixby Cooper of Michigan State University, John Coyle and Lloyd Rinehart of The University of Tennessee, among others, paid huge benefits. We participated in their educational programs, and they served as a great source of college interns and, ultimately, full-time associates.

We built a well-designed college intern program that included hands-on experience in order processing, inventory, and transportation. Students who spent two internships with us, and who performed well and demonstrated energy, enthusiasm, and a "team player" attitude, would be offered a position in one of our five regions. Our program called for new analysts to spend approximately two years in a rotation program that provided them with a substantial amount of operating experience. If they demonstrated energy, team play, and the ability to successfully execute their responsibilities, then they would be in a position to be considered for a supervisory position.

The fact that Integrated Logistics went for 15 years without filling a supervisory or management position from outside the company was a strong selling point for our recruiting program. We were especially proud to fill each of our director positions from within the organization. All but one of the directors had started as analysts at the regional customer service centers and had moved up through a number of positions, including regional customer service managers, so that when they arrived at their director positions they knew the business and—just as important—knew each other. It's not that there were no disagreements; in fact, there were many, but everyone always knew that the success of the team as a whole was the main priority.

Everyone benefited from this strategy of promoting from within, including the managers and supervisors who had to stay close to the business and the associates to ensure our objectives were being met. Building our team from within assured that we were all aligned in our mission and that we were, in fact a team. We demonstrated our interest and concern for our team players and rewarded them for outstanding performance.

Yes, we were creating our own culture—a culture within a larger culture of turmoil, second-guessing, and posturing. Throughout this book there are numerous examples, both direct and indirect, of the constant organizational churn and turmoil that took place during the years of mergers and acquisitions. It was a real pain in the backside, with some people acting less than professionally, which had a lot to do with the constantly unstable environment and pressure that was felt by many.

It is important to point out that our approach to management was to try, to the extent possible, to insulate our teammates from as much of the corporate "BS" as possible. Our goal was to make our organization a fun place to work, for our associates to enjoy their experience, and for them to have an opportunity to build a career in Integrated Logistics, working for the best of the best.

One of the most successful team-building events was "Rookie Night." During a regional meeting, Rookie Night typically was held in a private room at a local restaurant. The "rookies"—the most recent hires—would write and perform skits. Most of the time local and home-office management, along with regional associates, bore the brunt of the humor. Those evenings were a riot, with some funny moments that are remembered to this day. This practice helped a great deal in taking down barriers, either perceived or real. Good-natured ribbing followed Rookie Night. We conveyed a sincere message to all that we were a team, and that there were no sacred cows. We also made it clear that performance and leadership qualities garnered respect, not merely a management position.

I can remember one Rookie Night when an analyst named Rob Wodarczyk came dressed as me! He wore a clown costume, with huge gloves, huge shoes, and a very large nose. Well, I guess most of my friends know that I have exceptionally large hands for a guy my size and equally large, out-of-proportion feet. I hate to admit it, but my nose is also rather large.

Well, Rob went through some antics, told a few stories that I can't repeat here, and had the audience roaring with laughter. We were honored to have John Mitchell, a member of the senior management team I reported to, with us that evening. Every time I looked over at him, he was doubled over with laughter. Afterward John was very complimentary about the display of teamwork. He was aware of the team we were building and how we were going about taking down any barriers that possibly existed. What a night that was!

Getting back to how we not only survived but thrived throughout the corporate turmoil, a big reason was that we were a team through and through. The regional teams and home office worked together, ensuring that our focus was on getting the job done and not on politics. The team was secure in knowing what they were doing and how it was benefiting both the company and the team as a whole. Certainly there were debates and issues between the home office and the field, but they were amicably resolved.

As part of that culture, we had to demonstrate that when it came to hard decisions (e.g., personnel) the team would be fair to all parties. This reminds me of the example of a particular individual who had been around for a number of years but had difficulty keeping pace and didn't really understand the technology that was a necessary part of our operation. The team had to make the tough decision that, after going through numerous performance reviews, it was time to split ways. After an emotional departure, this person wrote a note expressing thanks for the opportunity to work with the team, and agreement and understanding of the action that had to be taken.

Creating a culture included the development of guidelines that were specific to our organization. For example, we expected everyone to be clean and neat. Things like forgetting a shoeshine weren't an option! We also asked for "gig lines" (a military term for aligning shirt, belt buckle, and trouser fly).

We never made a commitment that we didn't adhere to, or, at a minimum, we advised the other party when we couldn't keep it and when they could expect us to step up to the commitment at a later date.

We treated everyone, whether they were in sales, finance, manufacturing, marketing, or HR, like a customer. Think about it—if you expect respect and continued business from customers, then they need to be treated with the respect due them. By creating a culture where *everyone* was a customer, we gained their respect. Gaining respect throughout the corporation was a major accomplishment, especially considering that logistics and supply chain management were not considered to be important by executive management. To be recognized as *the* team that would deliver time and time again engendered pride in everyone. We knew there were outliers who didn't agree with everything, but we stayed the course and built one of the best teams in all of the industry.

There were occasional personnel and other problems that arose whenever a job the team did didn't meet our normal standards of excellence. There were all kinds of pressure on people, and some didn't handle it well. It was our responsibility as a team to show understanding and compassion. Our actions carried a message to the entire organization—we cared about our teammates. When the hard decisions had to be made, we would make them. Fairness and compassion went together back then, and still do to this day.

Politics

Politics reigns in many organizations, regardless of the size and structure. Whether a company is a for-profit or a not-for-profit entity, political persuasion affects and is pervasive in practically any relationship imaginable. Human beings are highly complex, and as such, individuals view subjects differently than their peers do. I don't pretend to be a psychology expert, but I have dealt with the machinations of individuals playing politics throughout my career.

Here's an experience I had when I was the southwestern regional manager for Standard Brands in the mid-1970s, around the time F. Ross Johnson was named chairman and CEO. We used a public distribution center operated by Trammell Crow in Dallas, Texas, that had previous experience with the Standard Brands business. The responsibility for inventory was managed uniquely: Accounting was responsible for the "book inventory," or dollars, and logistics was responsible for the cases.

After a physical inventory, before the days of the bar code, there was a 10,000-case shortage of Planters cashews. The value amounted to $100,000, and accounting insisted that the shortage would have to be reconciled or the distribution center would have to pony up the money. We counted, double counted, and went through everything several times, without success. A meeting was arranged in New York City at corporate headquarters, to be attended by the vice president of logistics, the vice president of finance, myself, and a few other team members.

The atmosphere was jovial, with the problem treated lightly. I was the new kid on the block, having recently been named regional manager; I was trying to read the players and decide what to say and when to say it. It wasn't long after running through the book inventory and hearing the opinions of those who were far removed from the issue that a deal was struck. I was to go back to Dallas and collect the $100,000 from the public distribution center. If it turned out that accounting was responsible, then the regional accounting manager would be terminated. If I messed up by not controlling the physical count, then I would be terminated. There were some handshakes, backslapping, and a few laughs shared. It was all about the political football being kicked back and forth.

I flew back to Dallas, ruminating the whole way. Upon arrival, I went to meet with the distribution center manager, with whom I had a good working relationship. He had worked countless hours on this problem, and he was completely confident that the shortage hadn't happened. Keep in mind that at that time, we were in the dark ages when it came to book inventory, reconciliations, etc. There were piles and piles of inventory reports that had to be threaded through, compared, and analyzed. While this was going on, the regional accounting manager in Chicago was confident that I was on my way out.

Within a couple days after I returned to Dallas, the distribution center manager called me with the answer. Accounting had mistakenly increased the book inventory by 10,000 cases of Planters cashews. The cause was simple: a keypunch error that had been made in the Chicago office.

This situation highlighted the fact that there were no controls in place to ensure accuracy. We took steps to implement "daily case control" at the DC and in the Dallas office. Each day, the starting inventory was adjusted for shipments and receipts, which identified what the daily balance should be, and this was reflected in the computer-generated inventory report. This program solved the problem, and it went a long way toward improving inventory accuracy and reconciling physical inventories to the book. Eventually it came to be used at all distribution centers in the Standard Brands network. The word that comes to mind when I think back to those days is "Neanderthal," or the way business was done 300,000 years ago! We took a giant leap forward that benefited the company.

There was a lot going on, and a long history of who held the trump cards in the company. Clearly logistics ranked at or near the bottom of the totem pole. This was but one example of the challenges we had to overcome as we embarked on the road to building one of the best organizations in the industry.

Oh, to complete the story: Chicago finally admitted to the error and for being responsible for the shortage. I was so relieved to put this behind us at last. It was more important to our team to know that we didn't make this important error than it was seeing what retribution was carried out. The story percolated throughout the company and our reputation was thereafter greatly improved, but it was just the first step on a steep stairway of challenges.

The most important criterion for manufacturing performance typically was the lowest unit cost produced. Consequently, when there was demand for a "C" item, it would most likely not be produced until it fit the plant's schedule—rather than produce it on a schedule that would meet customer requirements. Even though the distribution resource plan (DRP) clearly indicated the need for the C item, manufacturing might or might not follow that plan. Instead, plant managers might make a decision to continue to run a high-volume A product rather than break down the line and set up for a C item. I've seen that happen time and time again. Customers would cancel orders, and logistics would be accused of being the culprit. Having to hear negative feedback from customers, sales, marketing, and senior management was difficult when it wasn't our call not to follow the DRP plan.

Logistics has made huge strides over the years, even with few executives who understood what had to be done and who could round up the financing to build our supply chain management organization and supporting technology.

There are many examples of how politics play a role in the decisions that were made, impacting the effectiveness and efficiency of Standard Brands. I can't help but think about how Nero fiddled as Rome burned. There is a pecking order that exists, and it's very much a part of the politics game.

Leadership

It goes without saying that senior leadership's support is critically important. Without it, the foundation for developing the relationships and interrelationships necessary for collaboration to succeed will not be there.

These relationships are too numerous to list here, yet a breakdown in any one of them can lead to problems that will impact sales and profitability. Therefore, senior leaders need to promote a collaborative culture in which every company entity works toward the achievement of company goals.

Everyone has to recognize that it is difficult, if not impossible, to measure the level of collaboration taking place within the organization or externally with customers, third-party service providers, and others. However, the profit-and-loss (P&L) statement and balance sheet will tell a story that reveals the level of collaboration that is taking place.

I believe everyone in the organization needs to "drink the collaborative elixir" that will lead to an environment of teamwork and eliminate contentious relationships that do not add value. This evolution can start at any level of the organization, which then is considered as the "collaborative energizer," stimulating and educating the entire team. Advocates will step up to provide enthusiastic support while exploring the gains made by other companies and the path they took to success.

Trust

Trust: That which is critically important to the success of any organization.

Excellence as defined by Aristotle: "We are what we repeatedly do; excellence is, therefore, not an act but a habit."

In order to develop a culture that can be trusted, internally and externally, excellence must be ubiquitous, within the very fabric of every member of an organization. In every activity, a commitment made must be delivered upon, and every promise, be it formal or informal, must be met. Every member of an organization must always deliver, which conveys a message of excellence and trust.

Seemingly a small thing, but nonetheless relevant, is being in place and prepared for meetings, 10 minutes prior to the official start time. At Nabisco this became known as "Andraski time." Arriving 10 minutes prior to a meeting sent a message to other attendees that their time and their presence was respected. It is so easy to slide into a culture of always being late, for one reason or another, which is a sure path to poisoning teamwork!

Trust becomes ingrained and passed on to those who are new to an organization. Living the principles of trust serves as an example to the team as well as to those served by the team, internally and externally.

There is internal trust, supported by creating programs that ensure progress toward provide the highest level of proficiency. While developing these programs, it's critically important that company partners (manufacturing, marketing, sales, finance, etc.) are aware and have the opportunity to make their opinions and suggestions known and be acknowledged. Teamwork has to be inclusive to be successful in meeting the company's vision.

The most important aspect of external trust is to always create programs that exceed the customer's expectations. For example, my wife placed an order with Amazon for fertilizer that was out of stock at the retailers in our area. Within two hours of placing the order, she received a confirmation that the product had been shipped. The order was delivered the next day, and there were no shipping charges. This amazing performance will engender a feeling of trust in Amazon and raise the question as to whether it is easier to place an order on a computer versus making a trip to the mall or a local store.

Quality products, reasonably priced, that produce reasonable margins for the retailer and suppliers encourage collaboration. We also must recognize that logistics service providers should receive the attention and concern due them for the challenges they experience in providing the service that is expected. It's important to convey to service providers that you recognize the value of the role they play in meeting the vision of the company, and that their commitment to that vision is of critical importance. Delivering that message—that you want your service providers to be happy with the operational arrangements, and that you expect them to make a reasonable profit—is absolutely critical to forming a lasting bond of trust with them.

Change Management

A successful organization understands that, in many cases, change is hard to accomplish. That's why a successful organization makes an effort to understand change management and learns to recognize the barriers that have to be overcome. Underlying change is the importance of inter- and intra-organizational trust. Little progress can be made if trust is absent. Communication skills are paramount yet are often overlooked. When it comes to change management, communication has to be about not just "what" but also about "how" and "when."

My friend and colleague Prof. Lloyd Rinehart of the University of Tennessee has taught and written about change management for many years. He is passionate about education and understanding what drives sound decision making. I've included an essay he wrote on change management in the Appendix. It's good reading, and I think you will find his views offer a refreshing perspective on how decisions are made.

Few major companies have experienced as many changes, starting with the top executive suite and then cascading down through multiple levels, that Nabisco experienced. Because of the mergers and acquisitions that created Standard Brands, Nabisco Brands, RJR Nabisco, Nabisco Foods, and KKR Nabisco (the largest leveraged buyout of its day), big-time change seemed like a daily event.

In my opinion, one of the key drawbacks to all that change had to do with the impact on the associates, who were constantly trying to read the tea leaves to determine what was the new order of the day. Their reactions were many—treading water, reorganizing, searching for a new product or company to acquire, and finally to finger pointing.

Bottom line, with the exception of H. John Greeniaus, senior executives just didn't understand how to work within the matrix organizational approach that was used to provide Sales and Integrated Logistics service and expertise. It took a long time for the divisional heads of Nabisco Foods, Planters LifeSavers, and Food Service to get sales and marketing to understand the concept and how to work together.

Starting with planning, IL developed a three-year strategic plan that was shared with the senior executive to whom I reported. Frankly, I doubt that it got any more visibility, and I don't remember meeting to discuss it. Based on information shared by my superior, it seemed that whatever pertained to IL was considered to be at a low level of importance.

There was a lot of interest in what we were spending, and where and how cost could be mitigated. And while an IT task force was created, which I headed with a member of the sales team, I never got the feeling that we received the full commitment to be the best that we could be. In other words, no one was interested in IL becoming a superior organization.

I know that we succeeded through pure force and energy to excel in every aspect of the business for which we had direct responsibility, as well as other areas, including sales and marketing.

While senior management may have brought in top-flight consultants to review other operating departments, that was under wraps as far as I was concerned. However, I did work with Accenture, Cleveland Consulting, and Mike Hammer on projects to evaluate our level of proficiency and how well we prepared for the future. In each case, IL received high marks for customer service levels, competitive cost structure, and preparing the company for the future.

Educating senior executives was key, inasmuch as their knowledge of IL revolved around transportation, warehousing, administration, and inventory, and was rather perfunctory. But then again, for the most part they were compensated on sales and hitting their budget projections. Once we were near to or on the same page life became much easier to navigate.

I took great pride in managing change within my sphere of influence. My success was due in part to Integrated Logistics' organizational structure, and how all entities understood their interrelationship with other functional areas. I was recognized as having change management skills, and consequently was asked to manage the reorganization of the sales department (not including Biscuit or International). I've included an outline of that experience, as its results were nothing short of fantastic.

Case Study: Nabisco Sales Reorganization

From 1990 to 1995, the Nabisco warehouse-delivered sales organization had grown due to a number of mergers and acquisitions that had taken place. It was struggling in some ways as a consequence of blending the new businesses with the existing portfolio. The organization learned that making major changes at the onset of integrating a new company without a well thought-out plan caused serious disruption, which resulted in lost sales and, more importantly, dissatisfaction on the part of the trade. This negatively affected not only the products of the newly acquired company but the mainstay Nabisco products as well.

There is no doubt that mergers and acquisitions require a plan of action—that is not major news! What also needs to be recognized is that it is people who make up the company infrastructure. These people have feelings—strong feelings of self-preservation—that come along with any merger and/or acquisition. Consequently, they may not be motivated to ensure the merger is successful.

From personal experience with Nabisco's own merger and acquisition, I can tell you that the numerous steps taken in buying and selling businesses often take place at the drop of a hat. Companies could be bought and sold within days. This had major consequences for our group. For example, a liquor company was bought and its product stored in a distribution center that wasn't authorized to inventory liquor.

We were told to separate it from the regular inventory, rope it off, and take daily inventories. This went on for over half a year, and then the company was sold. This example makes the point that dealing with this type of situation takes team members away from their primary responsibilities, which ends up having negative repercussions.

Compounding this with several other decisions resulted in stress being placed on operations people to manage the exceptions and the business that constituted the company's infrastructure. What we experienced time and time again was an insistence by the acquired company's management teams that their marketing programs had to be continued; their orders (going to same customers as Nabisco's) had to be shipped separately; the functionality of their order management, sales reporting, and other systems had to remain; their personnel programs, including salary and bonus programs, had to continue … and the beat went on and on.

Until the differences between the companies were resolved, there was an impact on our ability to meet the high level of expectations we had established for ourselves. We were so good at performing, and we expected that the same level of performance would continue. The stress and frustration was palpable as we tried hard to be team players and have collaborative conversations with the new company. Dealing with the pushback, day after day, was difficult, but eventually the end game was realized. At times, the smaller, acquired companies acted like they were in the driver's seat and we had to acquiesce to their demands. What an amazing experience. I can only surmise that they were being told by their management that they needed to do whatever possible to make their company successful.

Under those circumstances, the cost of sales, as a percent of sales, increased to almost 12 percent—double the industry average. Furthermore, we were consistently missing our sales budget and what we were telling Wall Street. This led senior management to demand that action be taken. It was obvious that major, perhaps painful change— i.e., rationalizing the sales department—had to happen. This led to the following change management program, over which I had primary responsibility:

Step 1 was for senior leadership to explain to employees the challenge the company faced. Action had to be taken to get costs in line and to start hitting the sales budget.

Step 2 was to recognize that successful change begins with the people at the lowest level, not just with management. People can buy in and ensure success, or they may find a way to scuttle the plan. When faced with losing their jobs, their reactions are not predictable.

Step 3 was to develop and communicate the plan for making the change to all affected employees.

Step 4 was to kick-start the plan with a management team meeting led by an individual with change management experience. Teams were then assembled that included:

- Sales, with a focus on a sales organization with a bonus/incentive program to be in effect at a specific salary level.
- Technology needed to support sales planning, sales performance, etc.
- Marketing affecting the organization, cooperation with customer marketing, etc.
- Compensation, benefits, and other related aspects. Developing the severance package was of paramount importance, as a significant number of employees would be affected.
- Customer service, which would deal with order processing, order visibility, invoicing, and other aspects related to meeting customer expectations and working with sales.
- Logistics areas that would be impacted.

Each team was cross-functional (for example, people from sales, marketing, logistics, procurement, manufacturing, and finance). This ensured that a holistic, unbiased plan would be developed for each area identified.

Individuals were chosen by department leaders after receiving an explanation of their participation in the committee and the critical importance of their complete commitment to the success of the change management team. All of the teams came together for a group meeting, where they were addressed by a member of the senior leadership team. The major message delivered was that Nabisco Brands would not be able to successfully compete with a cost of sales that was double the industry average, and that sales would have to meet or exceed what was forecasted and supported by marketing.

From this inspiring and important message, the teams then met separately and were asked to:

- Develop the committee's mission, with a focus on how the team would feel about its work and the contribution it would make to the overall success of the change management program.
- Establish team goals that would be clear and achievable—there would be no "pie in the sky" expectations set!
- Understand and codify the challenges the team would face and how each challenge would be satisfactorily addressed.
- List the resources the team would require (information technology, HR, etc.)
- Identify the intended outcome and the impact on all associates, including sales representatives, sales management, and clerical.
- Acquire customer intelligence in order to adequately plan; for example, market share enjoyed by retailers, retail verticals that were growing or declining, and what emphasis would be placed on each.
- Evaluate the impact of direct sales vs. broker sales. This was of particular importance, as the sales organization had grown as a result of a number of management positions being created for the acquired company.
- Develop a calendar for meetings and dates to report progress to the change management leadership team, and then to senior leadership.
- (This applied to HR.) Craft regular updates to the sales force, keeping them informed of the progress being made and setting expectations as to when the project would be completed. The entire company also received updates on the status of the project.

The change management strategy proved to be very successful in convincing the sales force that senior management truly cared. The severance package was substantially enhanced to include early retirement opportunities, help in writing résumés, looking for other opportunities within the company, providing references, and other assistance for the sales associates and support groups. This approach was well received. The sales organization vigorously embraced this "caring plan," and the productivity level dramatically improved.

The end result was that cost as a percent of sales dropped below 6 percent within nine months of the start of the change program. At the end of the calendar year, an aggressive sales budget was exceeded by several percentage points. It's important to note that the organization, including both those who departed and those who remained, felt good about their company and how everything was handled.

A Path to Effective Team Building

Proper team building is one of the underpinnings of success for any company. I had a great opportunity when I joined Standard Brands to demonstrate my managerial and teambuilding skills. This wasn't included in my job description or evaluated during my annual performance reviews, which were all about the typical goals and objectives centered on cost and service. Yet to me, it was about building a team, centered on camaraderie and helping my staff improve their skills and capabilities.

I can say with confidence that Nabisco's Integrated Logistics organization truly understood what team building was all about. It is amazing that even after Kraft acquired Nabisco in June of 2000, this team—even after some individuals went on to work for other companies—stayed connected through the Nabisco Alumni group. The reason for this continuity is that everyone was made to feel involved and important during their time with Nabisco. We had fun while driving ongoing gains in service and productivity.

I can't point to a particular mentor who has had an impact on my thinking about teams or on what course of action I took to build a team. Frankly, I can only recall working for certain individuals who reveled in creating antagonistic circumstances among their peers and then engaging in debates. It seemed apparent that they truly enjoyed going up against other executives in the company, and that by winning those debates solidified their positions of power. They didn't really have any concern for building relationships or a team atmosphere across the company. Their main focus was on themselves and only themselves.

So I guess l learned what *not* to do, and I followed my instincts insofar as team building was concerned. To that end, I have always enjoyed getting to know associates within our group as well as other colleagues throughout the company.

Here are a few recommendations about team building that I would like to share with you.

Set an example
It's really important to set an example, and to be a role model that the team can look up to and feel proud of. Showing up in the morning before regular office hours is one sure way of sending a message that you are in it for the team. Always be one of the first to arrive at meetings, and be

attentive to the subject without dominating the conversation. That sends a message that you have confidence in the team to carry the ball.

Show you care

With each of the following you are conveying the message that you care! It is very important that associates know that you care about them as individuals and that they are making a contribution to the success of the company.

- Get to know people by walking around, with a smile on your face, and finding subjects to kick around in conversation. Try to find a subject you can develop into a long-term dialogue. This suggestion doesn't apply just to the home office but also to plants, distribution centers, regional sales offices, and any other company facility you're responsible for or involved in. This in and of itself sends a clear message to everyone, first, that you care, and second, that you are interested and want to hear firsthand what's on their minds and any suggestions they may have.
- Personalize the discussion by asking questions about the interests and hobbies of those you come in contact with; following up with comments and related ideas is a true value-add. I learned what specific individuals were working on, and I could then ask for an update on progress being made (or not). This always left an impression that I cared and had interest in them as individuals. You just can't put a value on that kind of relationship.
- Sports always provides great fodder for discussion.
- Celebrating company wins with impromptu get-togethers, topped off with pizza and soft drinks, is an enjoyable way to cement relationships.
- Celebrate holidays of all kinds.
- Ask for advice on a particular subject, be it a company challenge or something with broader impact.
- Always offer a smiling hello and/or a "high five"!

Finally, it's important to engender a sense of pride on the part of all associates to help them realize their full potential. Crafting and sending personalized, handwritten congratulatory notes to team members work wonders. Sharing progress reports written by team members with senior management is another key to building pride, because it lets them know that their work is recognized and appreciated.

Build a strategy/business plan together

When you are tasked with developing a business or strategic plan, you will achieve the greatest success if those who have a stake in it are allowed to have a say. They also need to know what might be happening soon! That's why it's important to do the following:

- Include as many members of your team as possible when working up your business plan as well as plan updates.
- Establish a reward program that recognizes team contributions.
- Be very clear when establishing salary-increase criteria that are tied into achievements laid out in the business plan.
- Budget for salary increases and bonuses based on measurable performance.
- Constantly find improvements in productivity to offset increases in administration and operating costs.
- Keep as many associates involved as possible. This allows them to have a good feeling about the experience and enhances their confidence in themselves, their associates, and the management team.
- Set a relatively short time line to begin and complete the business plan. An extended time line invariably results in a loss of interest and diminishes the possibility of success.
- When the initiative is completed, it's time for a celebration! Always remember to celebrate wins.

Always keep in mind that people do what they get paid for, and if they can find other opportunities that bring in the compensation they seek, they may leave if staying on is all about money.

Be a good leader

Team members will find great satisfaction in being part of an organization that takes the lead in making meaningful change happen. Everyone wants to associate with a winner and be part of a dynamic organization, rather than be a follower. This enhances their individual reputations, and collaboration with their peers enhances their opportunities both within and outside the company.

There is a lot that goes into team building, and there is no common path to success. Teams are made up of individuals, and all of them have their own values and ideas about what is important. It's the leader who has the responsibility of finding the common thread that binds them, and for getting people to work together to be the best that they can be.

So it is up to the leader to find the "magic glue" that will bring everyone together in spite of the most dire circumstances. If you believe it can be done, whatever "it" might be, you can do it! Believe in yourself and your team, and you can make it happen.

Chapter 5: Highway to Collaboration

Nobody wakes up in the morning and decides to collaborate, but the spirit of collaboration is intrinsic in each individual being. If you understand the essence of collaboration and reach out to cement communication and processes, driving everyone involved toward a common goal, you'll be successful. It's a worthwhile effort, because collaborative organizations realize substantial benefits exceeding those of competitors that believe in muscle building and flexing to achieve their goals.

I've been passionate about collaborative business practices for a long time, ever since we signed Nabisco Foods up for the collaborative program championed by Robert Bruce, who was a director with Wal-Mart Stores. He and Ron Ireland, who worked with Robert to develop the Collaborative Forecasting and Replenishment concept, shared what they had developed and their real-world experiences with VICS (Voluntary Interindustry Commerce Solutions Association; as noted previously, VICS merged with GS1 US in late 2012).

I was encouraged to join the VICS collaboration committee meetings by Ralph Drayer of Procter & Gamble (P&G). Ralph led P&G's collaboration program, with Wal-Mart being its first customer.

I had known Ralph for a number of years and always admired his ability to look into the future and envision the way things could be, and then do something to make it happen. Ralph and I agreed that to be successful, the program had to include forecasting, so we requested that the committee be named the Collaborative Planning, Forecasting, and Replenishment Committee, or CPFR. VICS then trademarked it as VICS CPFR® and we were off and running.

In this chapter I'll share some of my experiences with collaboration at Nabisco, both with internal departments and customers and with external trading partners. We'll also cover what makes successful collaboration possible, and how collaborative initiatives like CPFR® and Efficient Consumer Response (ECR) paid off for our company.

Collaboration Achieves Great Things

In every initiative—whether it is within a business entity, with trading partners, with technology solution providers, or with third-party logistics providers—it is essential that a spirit of collaboration be established. The steps to establishing a collaborative relationship must be thoroughly understood, starting with researching case studies that demonstrate what action was taken, the value that was gained, and the barriers that had to be overcome. Business drivers (promotional programs, targeted marketing, big data, etc.) must be taken into account and understood as well. And, of course, engaging and getting the support and buy-in of senior executives is critically important.

I have the great fortune to have been employed by companies where we were able to embrace new technology on one hand and processes that improved customer service and company profitability on the other. We would never have progressed as far as we did in those areas without collaboration.

One example that immediately comes to mind occurred after the acquisition of RJR Nabisco by Kohlberg Kravis Roberts & Co. (KKR). As mentioned in a previous chapter, John Greeniaus, our CEO, approved a $25 million request to build a forecasting system. We partnered with another organization that was experienced in building forecasting systems through a joint ownership program that included a "frozen" period, during which neither company could sell its interest. After that period expired, the system was sold to a software company that used it to build a very successful business.

The point here is that with internally developed knowledge we were able to build leading-edge technology during very demanding and trying times. What made it possible to bring together the necessary talent was management's recognition that it takes a collaborative state of mind and willingness to bring together team members from various functional areas to make progress happen. For example, the executives leading supply chain and technology developed the technology plan together, deciding what would deliver the greatest value over the shortest period of time. An unintended but beneficial consequence was the formation of teams that learned from each other. The team members were so well integrated that it was impossible for the uninformed to know who on the team was from which area—logistics or information technology.

The team's combined knowledge was greater than that of its parts, resulting in the development of leading-edge operating systems. The results showed up in company metrics: customer order-fill rates, customer case-fill rates, on-time delivery, and perfect order (on-time delivered and perfect order fulfillment). There were other measurements as well: sales per associate, cases shipped per associate, average shipment weight, transportation expense, warehousing expense, etc.

This holistic measurement system provided management with a system-generated reporting process that could be used to determine metrics by company division, by customer, by sales region, and by other views into the business. This information was relevant, useful, and effective, and it resulted in the logistics organization being rated among the top retail suppliers in the industry by several leading consulting firms. This gave the logistics organization a platform of pride and confidence that continued to drive gains in performance and company profitability.

Internal Collaboration Pays Off

To be effective at collaborating with a customer, we had to have a collaborative culture within our Nabisco organization. That meant starting with the development of a team, a real team that had individuals working together within and with departments in the Nabisco Sales and Integrated Logistics (S&IL) organization, and then on to sales, marketing, manufacturing, and finance.

Sales
The logistics team made an effort to connect with sales, and that helped to achieve a level of understanding that resulted in dramatically fewer order errors and improved customer service. Many order problems were exceptions that were typically channeled to sales, taking time to resolve and time away from selling.

It was a multi-phased educational problem, including transportation providers, distribution, the customer service department, and sales. Getting everyone on the same page, with the same understanding, made a dramatic difference in service levels and relationships with customers. When looking at the cycle, this relationship results in reduced product returns and deductions, contributing to the bottom line for all participants. Collaborative relationships resulted in improved business transactions, which translated to increased sales!

We engaged Professor Don Bowersox and his colleague Bixby Cooper of Michigan State University to write and deliver an educational program to our sales and management team. When I recently reread the document they prepared some 25 years ago, I was amazed at the relevancy that it still has today! Their understanding of the role that sales and marketing play in meeting customer requirements, and of the challenges faced by integrated logistics was key to the success of the program. John Coyle, Professor Emeritus at Penn State (now with the PSU Center for Supply Chain Management), also played a key role in our educational program.

Marketing
Clearly, marketing played a substantial role in everything from forecasting to sales and logistics performance to achieving profit objectives. It is easily forgotten that marketing has a dramatic impact on a company's ability to meet customer expectations—through new and exciting advertising programs, pricing, promotions, and products. Connecting marketing with the customer is one of the keys to success. So is educating the marketing machine.

Forecasting typically is the responsibility of junior marketing associates, who are new to the business and lack experience. Working closely with the new associates is important to the genesis of the marketing plan. For example, understanding manufacturing capacity is important, as it is absolutely critical to the success of the forecast! If there are prospects of selling more than can be produced, the company has to implement an allocation program that assigns specific amounts to customers, attempting to equally distribute the available product.

Our strategy was to assign a responsible individual to help manage a product group. This included understanding plans for inventory management, the flow of product, and working with manufacturing. The connection with marketing was an absolute necessity and resulted in a team effort. This one-on-one arrangement between logistics and the marketing person resulted in a strong, personal relationship that created a better understanding of what needed to be accomplished to meet the objectives of the company.

From my personal experience in customer marketing, it was clear that there was a gap between what manufacturing could produce (in what quantities and when) and the demands being made by marketing management. For example, two products that were produced at one plant were included in the marketing promotional plan and were to be sold in the same time frame. It was impossible for manufacturing to meet those expectations because the plant could only produce one at a time. Without intervention, sales would have sold in the program, and the customer would have experienced product cancellations.

Manufacturing
Linking manufacturing into the company strategy is easy to achieve if enough time and effort are expended. One of the challenges is to address the productivity goals that manufacturing has established for a given year. Those challenges typically have to do with long production runs of A products (core products), followed by B and then C items, which are the laggards. Some companies have a policy of discontinuing a C product for every new product introduced, maintaining the same stock-keeping unit (SKU) total. This results in improvements in every aspect of the company's supply chain. However, only a few companies understand just how much streamlining their product offering would positively impact their manufacturing productivity.

We had one experience that dramatically highlighted the importance of manufacturing understanding and complying with the plan coming out of distribution resource planning (DRP), which should be used to drive manufacturing resource planning (MRP). In this case, there were a number of customer order cancellations taking place, which impacted the division's forecasted sales. During the course of a meeting we were able to compare the products that were being requested from manufacturing and what was actually produced. It was readily apparent that manufacturing had decided to produce the products that had long runs and low unit-production costs. The products that should have been produced were treated as C products. Suffice it to say, the president of the division understood the problem and walked away in a huff, calling for a meeting with his own team. The point had been made, at least within one division of the company.

Procurement

The focus on procurement as an important aspect of the company's supply chain has increased dramatically. The opportunity to reduce raw material and packaging material costs is there for the taking if key information is shared and goals are put in place. When Nabisco, with the support of the CEO, turned its attention to procurement, inventory carrying cost was reduced by some $60 million. This newfound reservoir of funding allowed for the advertising and marketing of products that had been long forgotten by sales and marketing. Products such as A1 Steak Sauce and Grey Poupon mustard were soon seen in national television campaigns, which had an immediate, positive impact on sales.

Finance

Finance is also a very important cog in the wheel of success. An effort to educate the finance team can deliver important results for the company. For example, decisions to open or close distribution centers, change service areas, or identify what is going to be produced and where all need to be discussed with finance, since it is the keeper of the company "gold" and is directly accountable to senior leadership. So it needs to be included in an open discussion of any changes that have a direct financial impact on the company, with a detailed explanation of the rationale.

This approach will cement a relationship and communicate the importance of the finance group to the company's success, while opening the communications door for ongoing discussions. This is of critical importance before each sales and operations management meeting, since getting everyone on the same page will demonstrate team play to the senior leadership, resulting in an atmosphere of trust.

External Collaboration

Of course, collaboration was not just an internal matter. The contribution made by the transportation providers, public distribution centers, co-packers, and other service providers cannot be overstated. We worked as a cohesive team, each understanding our own roles and responsibilities. Our relationships were developed through strong communication and a desire to succeed at each level of the organization.

We supported our relationships by providing annual supplier awards at a joint Nabisco Sales and Integrated Logistics/service providers meeting, where we also promoted supply chain education. Underlying the "glue" that bonded us was an understanding that the third-party providers were entitled to make a profit! Driving down operating costs at the expense of the third-party providers was not a logistics priority, but expecting to be treated fairly was. At the same time, we worked with our providers to change business practices so as to improve their productivity. It was a very successful, win-win strategy that went far beyond what existed at the time and more than likely set a precedent for others to follow.

ECR: The Beginning of a Retail Collaborative Program

Now we're going to spend some time on Efficient Consumer Response (ECR), one of the first industry-level collaborative programs, and then on Collaborative Planning, Forecasting, and Replenishment (CPFR®), which was an outgrowth of ECR.

ECR was supported by senior executives from the trade and financed by trade associations. It was led by major corporations that committed a substantial amount of resources to the development of best business practices. I had the privilege of working on the ECR Operating Committee, which was a great experience. I had a role in reviewing, writing, and editing some 45 documents that are as relevant today as they were then. (I still have every one of them in my files, which my wife Regina has been after me for almost 20 years to send to recycling.)

ECR clearly defined the beginnings of collaborative thinking in the retail industry. It provided the genesis of Collaborative Forecasting and Replenishment (CFAR), and subsequently of CPFR®. In fact, CPFR® initially was an ECR initiative that was turned over to the Voluntary Interindustry Commerce Solutions Association (VICS), which registered the name of the concept and continued to drive the creation of a number of CPFR® scenarios that were made available to the public.

But back to ECR: In 1992 the Food Marketing Institute (FMI) sponsored a study that found that nontraditional competition—the low-priced retailers that focused on being the consumer price leaders, also referred to in the industry as "alternative formats"—were more efficient in supply chain management than the grocery distributors. These retailers used their efficiency advantage to gain a considerable amount of market share from the grocery trade, just as they did in apparel, footwear, consumer electronics, and certain other products. The grocery industry needed a way to respond to these more efficient competitors, who used technology and new business practices to their advantage. But grocery suppliers wanted to tread carefully, as they were selling to all of the retailers and didn't want to cause a backlash.

As a result, Efficient Consumer Response was born, with support from a number of associations, such as FMI, Grocery Manufacturers of America (GMA), and others. A working group of grocery retailers, wholesalers, and suppliers called the Joint Industry Project on ECR was created. It was interesting to note that all of the suppliers and manufacturers involved were concurrently selling their products to the grocery trade and to the nontraditional retailers, including Wal-Mart Stores.

The ultimate goal of ECR was to create a consumer-driven system in which distributors and suppliers would work together as business allies to maximize consumer satisfaction and minimize operating costs, while also making promotional spending more effective. Accurate information and high-quality products were visualized flowing through a paperless system between the point of manufacture to the checkout counter.

As a starting proposition, we defined what ECR was and what it was not, the relevant time elements, what constituted critical mass, the expected benefits, and the cost of implementation. Participants hammered out strategies, definitions, best practices, enabling technologies, implementation recommendations, and more.

The ECR strategies included:

- Efficient store assortments, to be reorganized around category management
- Space allocation based on accurate scan data
- Store-level sales history based on scan data, adjusted for promotional spending and seasonality
- Item-database accurate product information, to include dimensions, weight, description, and item count
- Point of sale (POS) consumer identification and demographics
- Reallocating space by category

Efficient replenishment was defined by:

- The integrated flow of both information and product within the grocery supply chain
- Store inventory, distributor/retailer inventory, and manufacturer inventory

A review of current best practices included:

- Store-level SKU forecasting and the promotional calendar driving the ECR forecasting model
- A consumer forecasting model with a feedback mechanism to constantly compare actual POS with forecasts
- Revisions to retail inventory targets and space allocations
- The roll-up of forecasts by store and then passing them Back to the manufacturer

Dynamic computer-assisted ordering, an emerging technology being used by select retailers:

- Should be forecast- and service-driven
- Forecast, plus store inventory model, plus dynamic computer-assisted replenishment (CAR) equals proper stocking level of each item per store
- Consumer forecasts, plus service-level targets, plus replenishment lead times, plus minimum order quantities equals retail model stocks and promotional order quantities

And the ECR program went on to include:

- Dynamic allocation
- ECR promotional strategies
- Recommended ECR trade-promotion principles
- Product introduction
- Test implementation
- Evaluation
- Decision between supplier/retailer to determine product and promotion
- Supplier benefits

The final plan also included creating initial ECR alliances, developing an IT investment program, creating a climate for change, and launching a program where pilot companies would define and share best practices.

In all, there were 47 best-practice documents written by industry experts, with information and guidelines that are still relevant today. However, ECR came along before the introduction of RFID for retail. If we connect the work of ECR with item-level RFID, the progress made by the standards organization GS1 in standards, "big data," the cloud, and the evolution of retail, then any company would have a winning strategy. Keep in mind that this kind of holistic effort requires collaboration!

Collaborative Programs Get Traction

ECR was well received in the retail and grocery industries. In late 1995, a Food Marketing Institute survey came up with these encouraging findings:

- There was commitment to ECR among manufacturers, brokers, wholesalers, self-distributing chains, and wholesaler-supplied retailers. There was commitment from top management, indicating that executives were playing a lead role in their companies' implementation of ECR best practices.
- Implementation of the ECR guidelines increased from an average of 42 percent to 52 percent.
- The total industry investment in ECR implementation in 1995 was estimated at $3.2 billion, an increase of 7 percent from 1994. Investment in 1996 was projected to be $3.5 billion, an increase of almost 10 percent.

It was commonly believed that ECR brought the grocery industry together as a response to the significant market gains that were being realized by Wal-Mart and Sam's Club. The point being that every major initiative has to have a motivating factor or be of enough importance that competitors would agree to come together to develop best business practices

A major goal of the Joint Industry Project on ECR was to help companies achieve critical mass and realize, as quickly as possible, a positive return on their investments in ECR practices and technologies. In the first progress report, conducted at the end of 1994, it was estimated that 8 percent to 10 percent of wholesale-supplied volume was being transacted using ECR practices.

Some of the issues that slowed successful adoption included inadequate information systems and information sharing between trading partners, which required top management involvement. In addition, a lack of the necessary skills and capabilities was a major impediment. Broader, deeper education and training would be essential to address these problems.

84

Considering what was taking place over 17 years ago helps to place today's challenges into perspective. While a significant amount of progress has been made—as evidenced by two examples of ECR-related multi-vendor consolidation included in the Appendix—the opportunity to take advantage of what we have learned thus far is substantial. (I wanted to say huge, but I didn't want to overstate our case!) The point to make here is that industry leaders, who are competitors in many cases, understood that there was value to be realized in coming together and developing business practices that would meet/exceed consumer expectations, while at the same time improving profit margins and sales.

Concurrently with the ECR initiative, Wal-Mart began its Collaborative Forecasting and Replenishment program (CFAR). This came about after Wal-Mart introduced cross-docking computer links to all stores and allowed 5,000 manufacturers access to data through its Retail Link system. The company then realized how critical it was to improve the accuracy of its own and its suppliers' forecasting.

The pilot program, which began in 1996, would validate a collaborative forecasting process, using a paper process (without technology). Warner-Lambert was the first pilot partner, and Listerine was the first product. It was a huge success. In-store service levels improved by 87 percent to 98 percent, overall inventory was reduced by two weeks, and Listerine sales improved by $8.5 million—the same impact as a first-year product launch—without the associated expense.

The success of the CFAR program stimulated a significant amount of interest in the trade. The original development effort between Wal-Mart and Warner- Lambert was monitored by Benchmarking Partners, SAP, and Manugistics (now JDA) from September 1995 to October 1996. It was transferred to VICS for stewardship and expansion in 1996.

VICS was created in 1986 by a number of large American department stores after they adopted the Uniform Code Council (UCC) bar code. They began to use the bar code to track products from origin to their stores and through checkout. This was a major change that resulted in approximately $13 billion in operational savings, as reported by the consulting firm Kurt Salmon.

The VICS model for developing business guidelines was to form committees made up of volunteers with specific expertise in floor-ready merchandise, logistics, and other areas. A committee was formed by a number of retailers, suppliers, technology providers, and consultants.

Shortly thereafter, it was agreed that, in order to develop a forecast, it's important to plan—ergo, CPFR® was born.

The VICS CPFR® committee published the Voluntary Guidelines in 1998, which included the nine-step model that served as a roadmap for implementation for a number of years. The committee, much like any organization, had its leaders, followers, and others who attended for a variety of reasons. Some were there to learn (but not necessarily to contribute), while others were there to connect with potential customers. By and large, however, the committee members were committed to moving the industry as well as their companies forward, and to improving their knowledge of leading-edge business practices.

While the nine-step model was important, we also learned that there were other areas that played an important role in moving forward with CPFR®.

For example, there needs to be a champion—a member of the team who takes the lead and is willing to devote the time and energy required to be the company-program champion, and to engage and get support from senior management.

Many of the CPFR® champions were not senior leaders, but came instead from mid-level management. These individuals believed in the ability to bring the company closer to the retailer—or in the case of the retailer, they became champions after struggling one too many times with out-of-stocks and forecasts that were far from accurate. Well, let's be honest: The definition of a forecast is "information that is intrinsically incorrect, supported by safety stock."

It is not easy for individuals steeped in the business practices of the past to accept changes that may be critical to the long-term success of the company. This is why this book spends time on the subject of change management—identified as the number one obstacle to successful adoption of CPFR®—as an important component of company strategy.

We also learned that when developing the CPFR® program "sales pitch" to the organization, and prior to taking it to senior management, all aspects of the requirements must be understood and in place, or plans to have the requirements in place should at least be under way. In addition, it would be critically important to have a case study (or case studies), endorsements from trading partners, and support from trade associations and academia to convey that it is an industry-backed initiative, which has measurable value to all the participants.

86

Collaboration: Turning a Negative into a Positive

Having been through my share of economic declines and financial challenges brought on by mergers, acquisitions, and leveraged buyouts, I lived through a time when cash was king, which meant that a substantial portion of net income went to satisfy debt while investors enjoyed a return on their investments.

During those hard times, we seemed to make some of our most important productivity gains. We had a great Nabisco Foods team composed of young and talented individuals. When allowed to turn their imaginations loose to generate new ideas, these talented team players came up with initiatives that made significant contributions by reducing operating and administrative costs while improving customer service, product flow, and working relationships with internal and external customers. We didn't call it collaboration in the early days, but that's exactly what we were exercising.

In a December 2008 issue of the *Wall Street Journal*'s Executive Briefing I read an interview with Harvard Business School professor Clayton M. Christensen by *MIT Sloan Management Review* Senior Editor Martha E. Mangelsdorf, which was especially relevant to what we were doing more than two decades earlier. Some excerpts from the interview are particularly interesting:

- The effects of the financial crisis and economic downturn will have an unmitigated positive effect on innovation. It will force innovators to not waste nearly so much money.
- One of the banes of successful innovation is that companies can become so committed to innovation that they will give the innovators a lot of money to spend. Statistically, 93 percent of all innovations that ultimately become successful start off in the wrong direction. The probability that you'll get it right the first time out of the gate is very low.
- If you give people a lot of money, it gives them the privilege of pursuing the wrong strategy for a very long time. In an environment where you've got to push innovations out the door fast and keep the cost of innovation low, the probability that you will be successful is actually much higher.
- Prosperity tends to insulate innovators from market realities and allows them to pursue their vision—a vision that is probably wrong, statistically speaking.

- The breakthrough innovations come when tension is greatest and the resources are most limited. That's when people are actually a lot more open to rethinking the fundamental way they do business.

The interview goes on and Dr. Christensen maintains this positive attitude as it applies to innovation, stock prices, and more. Dr. Christensen's views, supported by his impressive background, are energizing.

Innovation need not be dramatically new ways of doing business. It may be taking the time to understand what the current productivity inhibitors are and what can be done to remove the operational burrs. Creating and deploying unique and complex business practices while ignoring the standards and operating guidelines is a recipe for less-than-optimal performance.

Competitive advantage comes from unique products and a positive attitude toward consumers, customers, and service providers. Competitive advantage doesn't come from customizing software that makes it difficult, if not impossible, to maintain the software in top operating order. Being different doesn't add to the bottom line, while perfect execution of existing standards and business guidelines is the true path to distinction.

There may be steps in the short term that should be explored to reduce discretionary spending (e.g., travel restrictions, making fewer copies, etc.) but improving efficiency, effectiveness, visibility, and speed to market can be realized with what is at your fingertips.

Stepping up is about ongoing education at all levels of the organization, understanding possibilities, and taking ideas and case studies to management with a reasonable "go forward" plan that will support the company strategy. It is then that you very well may be at the leading edge of innovation and revel in the success that your company will enjoy and the satisfaction in a job well done.

There is no specific model that can be applied to business in general, but there are principles that should be understood and embraced, starting with those to be adopted by senior management. Number one is embracing collaboration. We all know that there are numerous silos that exist in organizations, each with measures for different goals and objectives. Across the board, a win for Department One may very well come at the expense of Department Two. For example, manufacturing

88

may focus on lowest unit cost produced for an SKU, not on producing the particular SKU that has been ordered by a key customer. The bottom line is that manufacturing gets costs under budget, but sales misses their budget and the customer is upset when the product isn't on the shelf.

The subject of silos is discussed in many venues as a deterrent to productivity. It's amazing that we continue to deal with the same problems over the years, but it amounts to a lot of talk and no real action. It's also amazing that the industry is lagging in taking advantage of proven practices that take more commitment and education than money!

Wegmans and Nabisco: A CPFR® Case Study

The following is a brief case study on CPFR® involving Wegmans Stores and Nabisco that demonstrates the value of collaborative business practices. This is just one example; I've also included in the Appendix a more detailed case study, contributed by my friend Larry Smith, about how West Marine benefited from implementing CPFR®.

As previously mentioned, the original development effort between Wal-Mart and Warner-Lambert began in September 1995 and continued to October 1996. At that time, the effort was transferred to VICS and the scope was expanded to include a broad consortium of manufacturers and distributors. A number of retailers, manufacturers, logistics service providers, consultants, and technology firms worked to develop a model for guidelines and industry roll-out. It was agreed that the results of the upcoming pilots would be made available through VICS.

A summary of problems the program's supporters hoped to solve using CPFR® included:

- Manufacturers' and retailers' forecasts are not integrated
- Manufacturers are not building to retailer demand
- Orders are mortgaged against on-hand inventory only
- Collaboration occurs only after the fact, when it is too late to solve problems
- Result—perpetuates "us vs. them" mentality

Thinking out of the box, the group identified the following potential actions that could lead to additional benefits for the retailer and the supplier:

- Single forecast across the value chain
- Committed/frozen orders
- Allocate supply chain capacity through production vs. on-hand inventory
- Pre-notification of issues in meeting consumer demand
- Common goals and metrics
- Capitalize on trading partner strengths

Retailer and supplier volunteers agreed to report the pilot results to the ECR "war room," which was managed by the supporting industry associations. The purpose of the war room was to provide consolidated results from the various pilot projects in order to share information and key learnings with the industry.

I can vividly remember Danny Wegman, the CEO of Wegmans, head of one of the most respected grocery retailers in the country and a primary driver of the ECR initiative, coming down the winding stairs in his Rochester, N.Y., office. He spotted me in the lobby and called out my name. I had an appointment with several members of the Wegmans management team; the meeting with Danny, whom I had met and worked with on ECR, was quite by happenstance.

Danny was very familiar with the guidelines we were working on, including CPFR®. We exchanged greetings, and then he asked if there was anything new and exciting happening in retail. I responded that I would like to share what I had learned about CPFR®, which I'd gotten involved in through the encouragement of Ralph Drayer, who was a vice president at P&G at the time, and my involvement with the VICS CPFR® committee. Danny said he was pleased with the progress made by the ECR Initiative, but typical of Danny, he was looking for the next big idea.

I took him through what Wal-Mart had shared with the industry and suggested that we engage in a pilot, with the stipulation that we agree to share the results with the industry. Danny's response was direct: Wegmans had no problem sharing their story, since it was the Wegmans team and culture of exceeding consumer expectations that provided the company's competitive edge. Given the steady growth in the number of Wegman stores in the Northeast and Southeast, it was a real endorsement of CPFR® that Danny was willing to commit his team to a pilot.

Danny asked me to arrange a meeting with the Nabisco team to discuss how we might go about structuring a CPFR® pilot. His team included Jack DePeters, Don Reeve, Mike Bargman, and Mike DeCorey.

90

After a review of what we knew about CFAR, and what we saw as the components and responsibilities necessary to conduct a CPFR® pilot, it was agreed to move forward with a CPFR® test with 21 Planters SKUs. We also agreed to the goals/deliverables, and developed key measures, the scope (functional activity, length of pilot, technology implications), and a communication process.

Danny agreed to publicly share the results of the pilot, which was another of the Wegmans contributions to moving the industry forward. This was February 1998. The next steps took place about a month apart: We outlined all initiatives between the Wegmans and Nabisco teams, created a joint business plan, created a sales forecast, collaborated and resolved the sales forecast, created order forecast/generate orders, set the delivery execution, and provided for an ongoing review and resolution of exceptions to delivery needs.

The second meeting was to produce process maps, identify key constraints, document a gap assessment, and set the action steps needed to close gaps. The third meeting reviewed the technology that would be required to move from pilot to production.

It was determined that the Nabisco forecasting system would develop the first pass at the sales forecast, and the Wegmans team would review it and advise of any changes they felt necessary. Nabisco would consequently make those changes and move them into the order forecast file. A key point to be made here is that Nabisco's technology had the ability to carve out a Wegmans forecast, for the 21 Planters SKUs, from the general sales forecast. We took great pride in our sales forecasting system, which gave us the ability to dissect forecasts by product, by customer, and by sales territory. This was a tribute to our IS team and their understanding of our business requirements.

The pilot process ran as follows:

- Planters only
- 21 SKUs
- Three months
- Start date of July 6, 1998
- Expanded to six months to include the holiday season
- Developed joint business plan, with third-quarter, July 4, and Labor Day promotions

Here are the third-quarter 1998 CPFR pilot results, calculated from the week ending July 4, 1998, through the week ending September 30, 1998.

Total snack nut category percent change:

- Unit sales +12%
- Dollar sales +17%
- Gross profit $ +12%
- Gross profit percent -.94%
- Sold on promotion + 31%

Planters Brand:

- Unit sales +36%
- Dollar sales +47%
- Gross profit $ +39%
- Gross profit percent -1.34%
- Percent sold on promotion + 43%.

The total weekly item forecast data:

- Total units forecast 113,734
- Total units actual 115,584
- Total difference in units/absolute difference in units 39,672
- Average forecast accuracy 65%

There is little doubt that the pilot was successful, as the decision was made to move to Milk Bone, a dog snack that had been in the Nabisco portfolio for many years.

Given the nature of the pet snack business and the annual sales volume, which was relatively low, expectations were not high for significant results. Yet the gains realized were in the 10-percent range, even with a minimum amount of effort. Planning together resulted in gains Mike DeCory described this way at a GMA meeting held in Chicago two months after we started the pilot: "It was like spreading magic dust on the products to be included in CPFR® and watching sales and market share increase."

We told the Wegmans-Nabisco story time and time again, in interviews, trade magazines, and at GMA and FMI meetings. Then it was time to move on, and Nabisco worked with a number of customers on a model based on our Wegmans experience.

I think it's reasonable to conclude that CPFR® was and continues to be successful, although it's not often referred to as CPFR®. A number of current trade magazines mention collaboration as being the glue that binds trading partners. It's safe to assume that the retail industry has "baked in" collaborative business processes. It is hard to imagine that the numerous new strategies in retail, such as omnichannel, could possibly be successful without this open-minded, cooperative approach to doing business.

Chapter 6: Building a State-of-the-Art SCM Business Model

Building a state-of-the-art supply chain management (SCM) business model begins with an individual who understands the value of SCM or, at a minimum, understands the individual components that can contribute to the success of a company.

Typically the initiative begins at the mid-management level when someone has taken steps to understand industry trends in business processes and technology, and how combining them can benefit his or her company. Benefits can be measured in increased sales, customer service levels, and improved profit-and-loss (P&L) and balance-sheet performance. There is no doubt that this is what senior management values.

Today many technology companies offer a complete package that includes enterprise resource planning (ERP) and other software that can manage not only a company's business but also how it communicates with its suppliers, logistics service providers, and customers. The challenge is to determine just what the requirements of each company are and whether the investment will achieve the nine- to twelve-month payback senior leadership desires.

Rather than provide suggestions as to how to approach this challenge, in this chapter we will take a trip down memory lane and use the experience of Standard Brands and Nabisco to help describe the key considerations and enablers for developing a successful SCM business model.

Order Processing

The Standard Brands Inc. (SBI) order processing system in the mid-1970s was, as at many other companies, in the "dark ages" in comparison to what is available today. The amount of manual effort required and the unreliability of the information were evident throughout the company. Each division had its proprietary system that was aligned with the accounting department that supported that business. There was no such thing as a corporate system. It just didn't exist, plain and simple. Fred Corrado, a member of the senior executive team, understood the need to move forward on the technology front and brought together representatives from Standard Brands Foods' northeastern logistics organization and an IT contingent led by Tom Gaughan, Bob Lyons, and Al Goodrich.

The team members came together to write the functional specifications for what they wanted to see within order processing, with IT helping to navigate through the technology challenges in terms of what was currently available and what would have to wait. Keep in mind that we were still in the age of teletype, long before e-mail and electronic communication. Getting customer orders to the plants and distribution centers was an ongoing technology challenge. It took approximately nine months to write the functional specifications and another six months for IT to complete the programming.

As we dropped the new order processing system into the five regions, one at a time, we carefully planned the training for analysts, the accounting groups, and others. Implementation went relatively smoothly, and even the old-timers in the regions could easily see the benefits in terms of ready access to information and the ability to quickly respond to sales inquiries and customers' questions.

This was a major accomplishment that demonstrated to senior management that we could deliver on a commitment and exceed their expectations.

Transportation Management

Transportation was largely ignored from an operational and systems perspective before and during the mid-1970s. Until transportation was deregulated in 1980, the traffic manager was expert, or presumed to be expert, in all of the tariffs, rules, and regulations issued by the U.S Department of Transportation, which had to be followed by shippers, motor carriers, and railroads. Transportation management stood alone until 1980. But then companies gradually realized that they could benefit by bringing transportation and warehouse management together. Thus a new entity called "physical distribution" was born. Both transportation and warehouse management grew in stature thanks to this important development.

Standard Brands' regional offices had very tight relationships with both the customers and the delivering carriers, and regional staff understood and helped resolve the customer service issues involving the distribution centers (DCs), carriers, and the order management folks around the clock. As my former colleague Al Yasalonis points out, NO ONE went home until ALL orders were covered! Yet carriers were selected and rates were negotiated by the corporate traffic manager and staff. Corporate held the "purse strings" for origin-destination lane general contracts all the way down to freight-bill audits. In those circumstances, our team achieved a balance by satisfying customers every day with regional service and "paying the freight bills from the corporate coffers," as Al puts it.

We knew that to place a renewed focus on getting product to the customer on time and accurately, we would have to move the decision-making responsibility for carrier selection from corporate to the regional customer service centers. The corporate traffic manager put up some resistance, and it took some time to get him to agree with and support this important transition of responsibility. The common ground between corporate traffic and the regional offices became the routing guide, which was an extensive list of carriers with corporate-negotiated rates. The regions could then pick freely from that list to deliver individual orders. This change affected a broad array of products (refrigerated, frozen, temperature-controlled, and dry), some 30,000 customer locations, and orders ranging from a few cases to truckloads.

Manually managing transportation was an exercise in futility, and oftentimes service was sacrificed for low cost. We had no information as to whether our customers were getting their orders when requested, and we were not aware of a problem until we received a call from the customer or from sales. The manual management system was designed to complete load planning based on inventory available at the distribution center, plant, or in-transit, and schedules for pool distribution or consolidation programs were refined by the team to serve several purposes.

We worked closely with our distribution centers, recognizing that collaborative motor carriers had an impact on the DCs' labor productivity for both inbound and outbound shipments. A narrower view of managing transportation would not have taken into consideration the distribution centers' cost of operation, but would instead have strictly focused on the lowest cost of transportation, since transportation represented some 5 percent of cost as a percent of sales, whereas warehousing or distribution center operations represented only 1 percent.

Our team took the initiative to develop the Logistics Order Tracking System (LOTS). This was a standalone system that captured shipment information from plants and distribution centers, including date, carrier, requested delivery date, and other mission-critical information. (More on LOTS later in this chapter and in Chapter 7.) The carriers were provided this information along with instructions to contact the regional customer service center if the requested delivery date could not be made and to also provide the reason why. If a delay was due to a customer not providing a delivery appointment, then the buyer was contacted and apprised of the circumstances. Then arrangements could be made to change the date or to provide the carrier with a date for delivery. The impact on the relationships with the customers and with sales was dramatic. Customers' needs were now being met, sales stopped receiving panic calls from customers, and we based our performance metrics on the customer's delivery date and nothing else.

There were some 60 pool distributors in the SBI network that were serving established geographical areas. Small, less-than-truckload orders (as small as 15 cases) went through this network. Planners combined orders of a reasonable size that could be stopped-off en route. That is, there were several delivery points on a truckload; each was assessed a stop-off charge, with truckload rates applying to all of the freight. Delivery dates dictated the planning decisions. Even with the extra $25–$75 per-stop charge for the smaller orders, the net delivery cost was better. Customers got on-time delivery and we saved money with help from the pool distributors.

Service was extraordinary and transportation costs very competitive. The working relationship that was developed with our carriers and pool distributors was based on our belief that carriers should enjoy a profit on every shipment. Operating reviews might reveal problems, identify the source, and then put in place an action plan. This was the logistics team culture: be easy to do business with and ensure that service providers enjoy a profit. This became the key to developing strong and lasting relationships that contributed to our ability to deliver and provide our customers with high levels of service.

Warehouse Management

Distribution center management was the forgotten child in the logistics department family. There were four privately operated DCs and 10 public DCs in the SBI grocery product network. All administrative work was done manually, and there were no common work practices or procedural manuals to follow. Products had a bar code printed on the shipping container, but it wasn't used in manufacturing, transportation, or distribution center management. The products were not stored optimally, and inspections constantly identified problems that had to be addressed. We had problems with stock rotation and filling customer orders with the right products. The DCs were crying out for reorganization and for operating guidelines.

It was clear that a DC management system was desperately needed in both the public and company-operated DCs. At that time there weren't any software packages that met our functional requirements, so we set out to build what we needed. We entered into an agreement with Trammel Crow to build out a system based on reading the bar code any time product moved within the distribution center. We gave the public distribution centers nine months to have a system with the same features and functions up and running, and we offered to share the information we had developed.

The results were amazing in terms of improved inventory, product rotation (the customer received fresh product and there was substantially less disposal of expired products), accurate shipping (reduced claims for products lost in-transit), customer order accuracy, and warehouse employee productivity. There were so many benefits realized that the DC team's esteem increased by the day. They were no longer at the bottom of the logistics organization; now they were real contributors to the success of the entire logistics team. Another win thanks to a collaborative effort by operating professionals, IT, and the public DCs all contributing their knowledge and expertise to the development of a state-of-the-art DC management system.

Inventory Management

We followed up with inventory management since it played such a critical role in every aspect of how we did business and related to the customer. Getting control over inventory was critically important, as it represented a lot of dollars on the company's balance sheet. Reconciling physical inventories with book inventory was an ongoing and costly nightmare, especially if a shortage was found and the public distribution center was asked to make a financial settlement. Rarely did records agree with those of the public distribution centers.

A new team was assembled and assigned to develop the functional specifications for an inventory management system. This team had to take into consideration the flow of information coming out of order processing and how to break it into buckets of customer demand, forecast requirements, and in-transit inventory. It was important, but it was a challenge to link in all locations of inventory, since plant inventory wasn't included in the information used by inventory planners at the regional customer service centers.

Suffice it to say, there was much to deal with in regard to flowcharting the information and bringing together the needs of sales, marketing, manufacturing, finance, and customer service. It was no small task, either, to deal with those who resisted changes to the status quo and everyday responsibilities. People tend to resist change and will challenge new ideas. We had to frequently step in and refocus them on moving forward rather than continuing to repeat the practices of the past. It was a long, drawn-out process to define what we could do—and needed to do—in order to meet customer and company expectations.

In many ways we had to set up the team like a think tank, bringing forth ideas that could deliver the expected results. We did a lot of research into what was taking place in the grocery industry at the time, but we didn't find the "magic" we knew we needed. The functional specifications were completed in six months and the system was ready in another two months. We were fortunate to have IT as part of the team that was developing the functional specs, because that helped to clear up questions that came up while the design of the system was being developed. This was a team effort, and all of the departments that would be affected were given the opportunity to review, critique, and approve the new inventory management system.

Labor Negotiations

As warehouse labor contracts drew close to their expiration dates, negotiations began with a meeting with union representatives and company management. Our secret "weapon" was Chuck Durney, an experienced and charismatic negotiator. As the lead negotiator, he established the game plan that would result in union contracts that were both fair and acceptable in light of the company's overall financial plans.

Chuck was a master of orchestrating every detail of the negotiating process. He left nothing to chance. He spelled out the role each of us— the regional customer service manager, warehouse manager, and private transportation manager—would play, including what to say and do, and when. For example, during the debate over a particular aspect of the contract, I was to voice my complete dissatisfaction with the direction it was taking, storm out of the room, and wait until Chuck came to get me. This plan was intended to convey to the union that there could be a serious impasse as far as management was concerned.

The result of Chuck's negotiating strategy was an agreement with the unions that satisfied the membership and helped to maintain a solid working relationship with them, improve productivity, and successfully implement new business practices. It was a true win-win at a time when it was difficult to arrive at a contract that met the company's operational and financial objectives while also providing the rules that would enhance the warehouse management team's working relationship with the union membership.

We learned so much from Chuck, who was clearly a master at union contract negotiations. Some of what we learned carried over to negotiating contracts with public distribution centers, transportation companies, and other third-party providers.

The Dawn of Data: LOTS and Data Management in the '80s and Beyond

While we're on the subject of homegrown information systems and how they helped SBI achieve remarkable improvements in cost, service, and product quality, I'm going to turn the reins over for a bit to Al Yasalonis. Al held several managerial positions within the SBI and Nabisco organizations. He played a primary role in developing our warehouse management system and LOTS initiatives. Al moved into various director-level transportation, operations, customer service, and inventory positions, and has since become a vice president in logistics and supply chain at other companies. I think you'll find his account of IT initiatives during the SBI/Nabisco merger period very informative.

We Were Serial Integrators

While the official merger of companies on paper is a thick contractual "signature" between corporate executives, shareholders, and financiers, the only true "merger" occurs once the inventories are physically merged, the orders to customers and their receivables are merged, the cross-functional organizations are merged AND THE VISIBILITY TO THE COMBINED INTEGRATED DATA is merged.

The lack of clarity about what data is available, and whether it is timely and accurate at *any* time, let alone during a merger, creates internal strife. It also makes it imperative to have external clarity. Customers want to immediately know who will ship to them and where their specific source points are for which products. How will the divergent systems talk? Simply, how will they get their stuff? In addition, vendors like third-party logistics (3PL) warehouses also need to know the where, what, and when for both inbound and outbound shipments. Is the new distribution network in a merger or acquisition understood and/or emerging? Specifically, who informs the customers of the emerging plans?

Company and major brand mergers can create incredible confusion across all parties, unless there's collaborative ownership of the ultimate data and sales communication flows. The emerging piles of data have to be converted to useful information for teams to use in their day-to-day jobs, otherwise chaos can ensue as individuals begin to quickly make their own assumptions for how the newly formed companies can be combined, often without desk-level clarity in the early days of a merger.

Even worse, a lack of data can lead to a lack of action. The early reports came out as simple data dumps onto 12 to 15 inches of 14-inch-wide, green-white "eye ease" paper that came off of clacking dot-matrix printers whose ribbons jammed daily. Dozens of functional analysts would attack that stack of reports like piranhas, with the goal of actually re-entering what they grabbed into VisiCalc or Lotus 1-2-3 software, because Symphony had barely arrived in corporate offices. Excel was a long way off, but we needed data transformed to real information to tell the story of that day's or

101

perhaps the month's business. We needed reports to make decisions. We were all taught that *information replaced inventory*. If data could be churned into information, we could reduce inventories at the distribution centers to gain the right "time and place" utility for the thousands of items. This process of churning order management data into daily decision information then generated inventory turns to benefit the top and bottom lines for our customers. Using the reporting to make the best decision was our mantra for success.

As the numerous Nabisco brands "met" the Standard Brands lineup in the early 1980s, the clash of "big data" (or our version of it back then) began, yet the emerging teams across the operations, customer service, inventory, and logistics functions yearned for collaborative visibility. If you think about it, isn't the latest enthusiasm regarding big data, touted by so many consultants, simply the 1980s version of integrating companies or brands via relational databases, but now on steroids? With the advent in recent times of secure server farms, software-as-a-service (SaaS) networks, and cloud-based Internet technologies, we are now providing what you could call the "performance-enhancing drugs" needed to accelerate the still-needed visibility at the core of business success.

"Big data" seems to be just the latest terminology for what collaborative businesses have *always* needed: decision tools down to the desks. Human nature has always created the need for desk-level data transformed to useful information, all the way back to the abacus in ancient times.

The rules of engagement, frankly, were not fully defined by our new leadership down to the all-important desk level. With any merger and acquisition everyone along the cash-to-cash touch points must redefine their individual roles, while senior management is simultaneously using high-level cash models to measure the performance of the integration. A collaborative gap can and often will be created in the critical transitional days. We had many questions ourselves, and seemingly even more questions came from our leaders, but we all needed better answers. As early as the mid-1980s we were asking how the Cro-Magnon data flowing from the early IBM mainframes to desktop PCs could be turned into real and actionable information.

It's important to note that Nabisco's multi-brand integration of business planning unit (BPU) relational data concepts also helped

102

pioneer U.S. pool consolidation for customers, especially those located east of the Rockies. In the late '80s, some 300 to 400 items across nearly a dozen billion-dollar major brands were going to thousands of customer destinations, combined on scheduled *shipment* days of the week so that *delivery* dates would be met, to the customer's continual delight! The shipping documents and daily data flows needed to follow suit. Out west, ServiceCraft (now part of Saddle Creek Logistics) was leading the way on multi-vendor consolidation. (See the case study in the Appendix.)

By 1985 the legacy transportation management systems (TMS) ALSO needed to accommodate this acquisition-related complexity through newly designed 14-digit bill of lading hierarchies. Each of the 14 digits' logic meant something to the distribution center ship points, down to order-pick configurations and all the way to customer final destinations far beyond the dozens of multi-state regional pool distributors. These dozens of regional carrier partner-vendors collaboratively helped to make the physical delivery dream a reality.

Nabisco perfected this process across five regions and the 48 contiguous states at a 99-percent-plus on-time delivery level by 1991. A system called DOCS (Distribution Operations Control System) was put in place to monitor that performance. We also used a tool called Fax Gate to automatically collect delivery dates from the hundreds of carrier offices across the regions. These details and related key performance indicators (KPIs) were meticulously tracked and reported, with extraordinary regional competition for accuracy. The results led to amazing company credibility and growth. Our regions and 3PL vendors trusted each other, and our customers trusted us.

Our logistics IT bunch began storing reams of order management system (OMS) data stripped from daily order management details in "stealth" fashion, on old IBM VM-760 systems at the Wilkes-Barre Data Center … usually around 4 to 5 a.m. to stay under the radar. Our logistics team did not yet have credibility with our official IT folks. We had to first collect the data, record it to the disk-packs, and then report it with field-record-level data validations down to the penny and tied to approved financials so we could develop and validate the overall proof-of-concept with the accountants. Once the data capture was finally accepted at the CFO level, the Logistics Order Tracking System (LOTS) was born. At that point, we all hit the ground running!

The collaborative teams thrived on the newly available and validated information reports. LOTS was tied to open and shipped order histories. Very soon, the Logistics Inventory Tracking System (LITS) emerged to capture daily item-level inventories from every stocking location.

Prior to LOTS and efforts at DRP/MRP into the late '80s, the CRISP (Calculated Replenishment Inventory System Planning) system also came to fruition. Our Integrated Logistics team was developing both conceptual and execution systems. While LOTS became the widely accepted tool, so many other reporting tools were under way. Again, it was all about getting decision tools down to the desks.

The team kept plowing away at the next cross-functional (OMS/WMS/TMS) "visibility" reports that so many of us were asking them to create. With common, accurate reports we could sustain the teamwork supporting our newly combined, multiple business planning units by major brands like Planters, LifeSavers, Specialty, and others.

New, tech-savvy logistics analysts learned to use the Dun & Bradstreet fourth-generational NOMAD language. These innovators teamed up to generate creative, solution-based exception reports. They looked at the emerging systems and were able to see order data in new ways that truly sparked senior managers to make new and better decisions. Our youngest analysts often made our senior people think by doing what Joe called "pressure up." That meant getting factual data to your immediate "up" supervisor despite day-to-day pressures, so that intelligent, nonpolitical decisions could be made. "Information is power," as they say, and the new databases made us powerful as a team.

In 1985 we also had challenges on the freight payment side. The transportation team began compiling the Cass freight payment information into a database (to tie to LOTS Nomad-type programs). The ARTIST (Ad hoc Reports Transportation Information Support Tool) front end for freight payments was simultaneously born.

We soon started saving hundreds of thousands of dollars across the regions with added Dbase III "Bernoulli Box" tools to control the freight bills, especially with the dozens of pool distributors and beyond bill of lading "details from hell." There were over 200 boxes of shipping documents that came into headquarters, while hundreds more were held in the regions. With the ARTIST freight payment-visibility system we were able to clear the decks. Carrier claims and piles of shipping documents dropped like a rock from high-six-digit dollar amounts to under five digits. Our clerks were happy not to hump boxes of BoLs around the office, and they became comfortable with screens that could still answer their intuitive questions. We felt electronic in the '80s.

CRISP helped start our path toward "geographic timed phased net requirements" (GTPNR). This is a term the internal and Integrated Logistics team used frequently, meaning that planning takes into consideration the geographic location as well as when inventory was needed to meet customers' delivery requirements. The LOTS, LITS, and ARTIST reporting systems were in place by 1987, and we also made time to improve our MRP and DRP efforts with Manugistics. New-product supply teams were linked to the business marketing groups, with a focus on optimal inventory management while managing ongoing product launches and merger-integration efforts. Just to keep the process-improvement efforts even more interesting, we launched a whole new WMS initiative by 1987 with radio frequency (RF) Telxon scanners. We implemented our own distribution center management system with Trammel Crow's help in 1987–88 across the four private DCs, starting with the "PRIDE" (Portable Radio Input Device Education) RF scanners program at Chesapeake, Va. We followed Chesapeake with Portland, Modesto, and finally, our largest DC in Bedford Park, Ill., while the other three DCs continued working out the kinks as they went.

Our team culture ensured that we kept sharing the programming guts and real reporting results. Eventually everyone was trained just enough to be dangerous when it came to the validated reporting we sent up through the executives, helping them make the next great decision. It was a healthy, internal competitive race to come up with the next cool report, and then install it and share it. Everyone worked in a true spirit of teamwork to run daily "watch for" exception reports. We had over 700 exception reports running each day by the late '90s, looking for needles in the haystack ... but only a dozen or so meaningful AND actionable reports would drop to the printer if needed (actually by analyst name) so that folks could manage by exception. Now *that's* visibility!

A Tribute to a Great Nabisco Foods Team

Al has done a terrific job walking us through the incredible improvements that resulted from the collaboration between the IT pros and the logistics team at Standard Brands and then at Nabisco after the merger. I'd like to add some of my own comments and compliments here.

IT is a strategic enabler if the systems are developed in concert with the customer—the individual departments within the company—to arrive at a holistic, easy-to-use software package.

The Nabisco experience may be a model to consider. The IT and SCM leaders collaborated! It was agreed that the functional specifications of any and all SCM operating systems would be the product of a team made up of members from both SCM and IT. A member of the SCM team, Joe Wisdo, had in-depth knowledge of Nabisco's business requirements and was appointed as a lead IT manager. He made a major contribution to any success that we enjoyed.

In my view, what truly separated the Nabisco Foods team from the competition was the head start we enjoyed on what was to become the new frontier of business intelligence (BI). Wikipedia defines BI as the collection of technologies, applications, and practices to improve business decision making using fact-based support systems. BI systems provide historical, current, and predictive views of business operations, using data that has been gathered into flexibly designed databases. These applications are used for such functions as demand forecasting, production analysis, customer service level measurement, and profit modeling.

Some of the names we have come to know over the past decade include Cognos, Hyperion, SAS, and Business Objects. While they each have their individual capabilities and unique qualities, they share many similarities regarding their ability to manage and analyze large quantities of data from disparate sources over long periods of time. One other quality these leading applications all share is that most were barely in their infancy when Nabisco Foods was using these same "gather, analyze, and report" techniques to improve its decision-making quality in the late '80s and early '90s.

I never really had the chance to work directly on the seemingly nonstop integration efforts that resulted from the introduction and exit of brands in the portfolio. I was fortunate enough, however, to be able to observe this team as they worked together to understand every possible byte of data that passed in front of them. Nothing was too insignificant to collect and measure, and as a result, nothing was incapable of being managed. The team embodied the principle that you measure what matters so you can effectively manage what you measure.

Another interesting characteristic of this group was that there was no distinction made between the "ops types" and the "data geeks." After a while, when the functional requirements team met, it was impossible for anyone who was not familiar with the team to determine who was with SCM and who was with IT. In fact, training on the use of LOTS was mandatory, and virtually everyone in Integrated Logistics was capable of accessing the database and reporting results in high-quality, dashboard-like formats to customers, service providers, and suppliers. Due to the highly changeable nature of our environment, the ability to spin, slice, and dice data into actionable reporting was not just a luxury— it was a requirement. The end result was a state-of-the-art SCM system that allowed Nabisco's warehouse-delivered products to be ranked among the leaders in this vertical.

Accurate Information

An assumption going into any business transaction is that the information on the suppliers' and retailers' product masters are in sync. In other words, the product codes, descriptions, package dimensions, package weights, and number of units are the same in each partner's product master. But anyone who has been in this industry for any period of time knows that there is a great opportunity for improvement when it comes to data accuracy between trading partners. They'll also be familiar with the problems that arise when data is out of sync—something that is regrettably prevalent. So what's a person to do when faced with this situation?

The answer is different depending on each company's circumstances. Some may try to avoid the need to assign a new item number (Global Trade Item Number, or GTIN) or apply for a new GS1 US product code by assigning a prefix or suffix to the base code—even when, for example, the individual units may be 20 percent heavier, and with each case weighing more, the pallet configuration is different than what is in the product master. Consequently, when load planning is being done, the change could, and in many cases does, impact what can and cannot be placed on the truck. This was something we experienced at Nabisco Brands. Our inventory was cluttered with prefixes and suffixes that were used to avoid requesting a new UPC number and incurring the associated cost. This presented an ongoing challenge for everyone, inside and outside the company.

There are several data-synchronization services that can be found on the Internet. Each has its own approach, and you should do a careful review and then choose a solution that fits your business model.

It's my opinion that a global solution that includes the Global Data Synchronization Network 8 (GDSN) that links a number of data pools to accumulate and distribute information is very valuable. Should a company decide to participate in the Global Location Number (GLN) program, there is specific information available on retailer locations (e.g., buying office, distribution center location, even down to the door). Combining several service provider capabilities provides an opportunity to share information and makes it possible to provide high levels of service. It also provides the retailer with information as to what products are offered by suppliers and in what geographical location.

This is not a commercial for any particular service provider. In my opinion we are looking for a holistic and all-encompassing approach to ensuring that information can be shared in a complete and viable business proposition that has proved to add substantial value.

If current business practices do not ensure that accurate and timely information is available and easily accessed, at a reasonable price, CPFR® cannot be successful. In fact not only will CPFR® be compromised, but every aspect of a company will incur unnecessary expense dealing with exceptions that will be the nemesis of productivity and efficiency.

Metrics

This takes us to metrics. It bears repeating: You can't manage what you don't measure. It's very important that the metrics are clear and that trading partners, as well as the trade, are in agreement.

Let's look at two examples of metrics that seem to be straightforward and in compliance with the relevant requirement but may result in problems. The first is "on-time delivery," which must be managed so as to meet the delivery date on the purchase order. Keep in mind that the delivery date on the customer order is determined by the retailer's replenishment system, which dictates when the product in question must arrive at the designated distribution center.

Frequently, carriers are unable to get an appointment from the retailer's distribution center to comply with the requested delivery date, so they take whatever is available. It is clear that if that's reported as an on-time delivery, it is incorrect!

The next metric is "order complete and case fill as ordered." Typically a supplier will substitute a product of the same description—essentially the same product—except that it may be a bonus pack that had previously been offered. This order will be reported as a complete order with case fill (e.g., 1,500 cases ordered, 1,500 cases shipped), yet this is inaccurate and misleading. The substituted product may not be of the right size to fit on the shelf, plus it's a bonus pack, which is not expected.

In the early days of my employment at Nabisco, top-to-top meetings between our company and our customers were frequently dominated by complaints about service. Often it was because our metrics disagreed with the customers' measures. For example, we called a substituted product a miss, even if the customer approved of the substitution. When it came to on-time delivery, we called the customer as soon as the carrier reported—through a homegrown Nabisco system—that the delivery couldn't be executed as the customer requested. We then would call our sales person and the customers' distribution center to resolve the delay. In each case we explained the situation, and the buyer would make the call as to whether or not to demand that the product be delivered.

These two steps, as well as others to ensure our metrics were in agreement with those of our customers, made a major statement that we cared enough about their business to make this change. Thus, it was not necessary to discuss service/metrics in future top-to-top meetings between management and customers. As important was the impact on our operations and method of communication as we became better aligned with our customers.

Actions such as these prepare a company for a collaborative program with the customer with an eye on improving forecasting and consequently meeting consumer expectations.

Time out for an important message: Keep the "keep it simple, son" (KISS) idea in mind. This is extremely important, because the effort to differentiate a company can easily create unusual and unnecessary system and process requirements. The end result is increased administrative and information system costs, with service failures added in for good measure.

Associations

There is little doubt that great value can be realized by becoming engaged with associations that are supportive of the development of industry guidelines. Some examples include the Council of Supply Chain Management Professionals (CSCMP), the Grocery Manufacturers Association (GMA), and the Food Marketing Institute (FMI).

I've been involved with a number of those groups, but I am going to focus on VICS, which Nabisco supported, and where I served as president and CEO for eight years. (VICS merged in 2012 with the standards organization GS1 US, but most of its programs remain active.) Individuals representing companies that participate in VICS programs can substantially benefit from the opportunity to learn from others who have experienced CPFR® implementation about the challenges they encountered in implementation, collaboration, and the use of technology.

VICS' dedicated members have delivered a number of enhancements since the original guidelines were completed in 1997. Just consider these industry-motivating documents produced by the VICS CPFR® committee: Retail Event, DC Replenishment, Store Replenishment, Collaborative Assortment, CPFR® for large-scale implementations, linking CPFR® and sales and operations planning (S&OP), and now linking CPFR® to DRP/Integrated Planning. Larry Smith of West Marine was the key driver and author of these thought-leading documents. Kudos to Larry.

Amazing leadership combined with strong participation by industry leaders has produced unbiased, technology-enabled business guidelines that can move the industry forward. There is no doubt that this level of participation proves the value of collaborative initiatives that can take place with passionate and devoted volunteer leadership. This committee set the precedent and is largely responsible for the growing interest today in collaboration.

Linking Sales, Marketing, Finance, Procurement, and Manufacturing

The many challenges that executives have to deal with include issues that can be best managed within an organization by departments that have common goals and objectives. However, based on our experience going back to SBI, Nabisco Brands, RJR Nabisco, and KKR/RJR Nabisco, we didn't hold out much hope of finding meaningful linkage, collaboration, and cooperation. Keep in mind that "command and control" was prevalent in the 1970s and 1980s, and it was the driving force for many decisions and attitudes about team play and cooperation. This is the environment that the management team grew up with, and they managed accordingly.

At Nabisco, some of the gains that were made were only possible because of the logistics organizational structure, which placed talented and experienced individuals in positions that encouraged them to interact with the marketing, finance, and manufacturing departments for specific brands. Working together to achieve the very best result created a team approach. It didn't come about because of a divisional president stepping up to champion a team effort to benefit a particular brand or brands. Sometimes when shortcomings were identified blame was incorrectly placed on logistics. In many cases, it was just an expression of frustration that each area did not have its own separate sales or logistics organization.

An organizational decision to form the Sales and Integrated Logistics organization brought these two functions together and resolved issues that were nonproductive irritants for years. The group became a team, with common goals and objectives focused on the customer. I don't think that there are many, if any, other companies in the retail sector that have taken the same approach.

Thinking Outside the Logistics Box

The question so often asked by senior managers when their approval is needed for an important project is simply, "So what?" It's important to keep these two simple words in mind when developing a capital appropriation request. You have to understand that senior managers have a lot on their plates and don't have the background that you do. Consequently, it's not important to extol the virtues of your proposal.

Instead, think of it in terms of how it will financially benefit the company. That will get their attention, I promise!

I have to add that your proposal has got to be realistic and achievable in the time frame laid out for completion. If there are any exaggerations in terms of a leap forward, your proposal will meet a sure and instant demise.

So, you ask, why do I bring this point into the conversation? My answer is that had we presented a plan to Nabisco Brands senior management that projected the tremendous progress we actually made, it would have been met with immediate rejection. They would never have believed that the accomplishments I'm going to tell you about could have been realized.

The following are some of the "out of the box" programs that Integrated Logistics created, and which contributed to the groups' remarkable success:

Customer service specialist, Key Account program, and customer-managed inventory

Customer service specialist: In 1989 we established the position of customer service specialist. We named three customer service specialists in each of the three regions and asked them to take on the responsibility of seeing that the key metrics of 25 customers were closely followed. They helped us come to be recognized as *the* company that provides high levels of customer service and was constantly identifying and taking advantage of service improvements.

Key Account program: The Key Account program was simultaneously enacted with 32 customers, concentrating on case fill and on-time delivery, with each closely tracked to ensure we were meeting/ exceeding our goals and those of our customers.

Customer-managed inventory: It became fashionable in the grocery industry for suppliers to develop and implement customer-managed inventory for key accounts. Our IS group developed the program that allowed us to establish programs with 12 customers in four regional customer centers. We quickly realized that the success of each program was largely dependent upon the analyst charged with the responsibility. There were substantial differences in the service provided to the customers in the program, which was something we successfully addressed.

112

This focus on customer service was not a result of a management dictate; it originated from the passion our team had to excel and from the understanding our team had of the trade. Involvement in FMI, GMA, and CSCMP helped us to build customer service programs And to understand how this focus would result in higher, more profitable sales.

Customer profitability

We decided that it would be critical to understand the profitability of each customer by product group. This system was developed by Tony Galli, our financial guru. We are indebted to Tony for his understanding of the challenges and the great system that he built. We also have to recognize the contribution of Steve Kingsbury and his team, Rob Wodarczyk and Marylyn Brown, who through their own initiative built the Logistics Order Tracking System (LOTS) described in detail earlier in this chapter.

The LOTS database was the backbone of the customer profitability initiative. Over time, LOTS evolved from just transaction-based logistics costs (transportation and warehousing) to include product costs (COGS), invoice-based trade promotion expense, and variable selling (broker expenses). Eventually, an approach was developed that assigned fixed expenses, such as fixed distribution (e.g., customer service), using a product- and customer-based assignment process, which was itself based on a series of metrics that replicated the complexity of various orders. Finally, assessorial expenses such as detention and unloading fees were extracted from the freight bill detail, and a true cost-to-serve picture for customers and products started to emerge.

An extract of the LOTS detail was loaded into a database with an Excel front end, and customer P&Ls were developed. These could be run for a summary of a retailer's headquarters location (sold to), or right down to the actual delivery location (ship to).

The information generated provided a defensible position for determining which customers warranted strategic investment (such as customer alliance programs), and for other customers, it identified behavior trends that could be addressed as areas for improvement. The customer P&Ls also provided a portfolio-based perspective of customers (retain/grow/sustain), which previously had only been used for product analysis.

Aged inventory

The amount of aged inventory carried in our distribution centers and plants represented a cost center that demanded our attention. Aged inventory was either disposed of in a land fill or sold as distressed merchandise. In either case, it was a cost to the company that needed to be addressed. Our focus on the rotation of inventory and identification of aging inventory had a significant impact, with a reduction from 688,000 cases in January 1990 to 205,000 cases in December 1990. This information was shared with all concerned individuals within Sales & Integrated Logistics and the business units.

Common order processing system and integration of Planters LifeSavers

By mid-July of 1992 we had successfully implemented the new common order processing system and smoothly consolidated customer service responsibilities for Planters LifeSavers into Winston-Salem. We were complimented by John Greeniaus, our CEO, for completing these two difficult projects, which had required a tremendous amount of hard work and cooperation to complete. We made this happen as a "family."

Nabisco Foods Co. and Food Service inventory

Emphasis on sales forecasting and strong inventory management practices reduced NFC out-of-date inventory of $94 million in January 1991 to $21 million in September 1991, or 18.3 percent less than the same period in 1990. This contributed to cash flow and the balance sheet.

Inventory of Food Service products was $28.6 million in January 1991 and had dropped to $23.6 million in May of that year. Case fill was at an all-time high of 98.2 percent.

Integrated Logistics distribution center management system

It was clear to our team that we would not achieve the operational and customer service goals we had set for ourselves unless we implemented a warehouse management system. After reviewing and determining that software packages offered by technology companies didn't meet our requirements, we entered into an agreement with Trammel Crow Distribution Inc., working with our longtime friend and colleague Cliff Lynch.

Given that we had a running start with the Trammel Crow system (from our warehouse management project during the Standard Brands days), we benefited substantially and added features and functions that our team decided were absolutely essential.

114

To that end, Alan Yasalonis led a cross-functional team from Nabisco's northeast regional customer service organization, Trammel Crow, and Nabisco Information Systems. The system delivered state-of-the-art operational benefits and improved customer service, stock rotation, and labor productivity. The results were amazing and the cost to build it was miniscule!

We then advised the eight public warehouses we were using at the time that they had to buy our system, buy a software package from a technology company, or build a proprietary system. They were given nine months to complete the project, or we would replace them with one of their competitors.

This wasn't an unreasonable demand, as we had addressed this subject for a minimum of two years prior to setting the target. We were able to use the immediate benefits we were seeing from our new distribution center management system to explain to them how the system would have a one-year payback, and that it would greatly enhance their competitive stance in the public warehousing business. Much to our delight, all eight of the public DCs accepted our challenge and had their systems up and running prior to the due date. Each saw immediate benefits!

Having each of our distribution centers equipped with a DC management system delivered additional benefits in terms of stock rotation and warehouse labor productivity. That resulted in lower rates, which meant lower costs for Nabisco Integrated Logistics. It also meant that there were fewer exceptions to deal with, and we spent less time managing distribution center problems.

Plant-direct shipments of dry products
In 1988, plant-direct shipments represented 1 percent of our customer shipments. Steve Kingsbury designed and implemented a system that allowed us to readily identify plant-direct opportunities and link that with the regional efforts to ship orders from the plants. In 1990, 7.27 percent of our customer shipments went plant-direct without customer incentives. That dropped $700 per shipment to the bottom line, for a total savings of $1.5 million—a solid contribution to the company's P&L.

National damage-reduction program/claims and disputes

This program, which was implemented in 1990, gave us the information we needed to address the root causes of product damage. Thanks to this initiative, Integrated Logistics dramatically reduced distribution- and transportation-related claims and customer disputes. For example, the claims balance for April 1991 was $150,000 vs. $275,000 year-to-date (YTD) in 1990. Disputes were managed down through the "perfect case" program from $162 for January through April 1990 vs. $146,000 for the same period in 1991. In April 1992, disputes totaled $130,000 and only $30,000 in claims was filed.

Top Guns in the Grocery Industry

From my days in Standard Brands' distribution organization through the formation and growth of Integrated Logistics at Nabisco, I was proud to work with people who took the initiative to serve the customer better while improving processes and profits. But, as you can probably tell, nothing is dearer to my heart than the Nabisco Integrated Logistics team. I hope the IL team members' dedication, technical expertise, and ingenuity are clearly evident in the examples included above.

There was much organizational turmoil and other factors that could work against building an organization and business model, and yet ours turned out to be one of the best. However, it's not like senior management sat back and didn't take our pulse from time to time. Several major consultants were assigned to spend months with us to evaluate almost every move we made. The late Dr. Michael Hammer, author of the best-seller *Reengineering the Corporation* and famous for his "blow it up and start over again" approach, sent his team to spend time with us, and their final report gave us high marks. Roger Kallock's organization, Cleveland Consulting, concluded that we were in the top three food-company supply chain organizations in terms of customer service and other metrics. We were endorsed at every turn by reputable consulting companies and kept on ticking.

More importantly, we were recognized as the best by our customers. In 1990, a Preferred Supplier Trade Survey conducted by NEO Corporation International Ltd., asked our customers to rate the leading suppliers in the food business on an overall basis. At that time General Mills led, followed by Ralston Purina, Kellogg's, and Quaker Oats. Nabisco was situated in fifth place.

Three years later, Nabisco was the number one choice of 49 percent of our customers, outscoring P&G, Leaf, Kraft/General Foods, Ralston Purina, Wrigley, Sun Diamonds, and Eagle Snacks!!! This was incredible given the many changes that had taken place since the merger of Nabisco and Standard Brands, and then Nabisco and RJR. Underlying Nabisco's dramatic strides in how the company was perceived by its customer base were a number of improvements that impacted the productivity of its customers. There was little doubt that Integrated Logistics and our colleagues in IT played a key role in this improvement.

Chapter 7: A Look into the Future

I am convinced that one of the main pillars of a comprehensive business management process is manageable and user-friendly technology. The right technology, properly applied, can make the difference between adequate and excellent.

For example, companies struggle with dramatic forecasting errors and other SCM challenges that are largely the result of inaccurate information. But by using technologies like item-level radio frequency identification (ILRFID), retailers in particular can make big gains in accuracy in terms of inventory tracking, demand forecasting, and other activities that impact their ability to have products on store shelves where and when consumers want them.

Those who know me know that I am passionate about ILRFID. I chose to name this chapter "A Look Into the Future " because I am completely convinced that this technology will, over time, replace the bar code, and it will have a major impact on supply chain management across all industries. A primary objective I have for this chapter is help the reader gain a better understanding of ILRFID, wiping away current misunderstandings about it and making the benefits of implementation clear.

This chapter will also briefly touch on omnichannel merchandising and its emphasis on providing consumers with the ability to order product any time, from anywhere, to be picked up from or delivered to the

118

location of their choosing. Inaccurate inventory information will truly have a major impact on a retailer's ability to meet the expectations of the consumer who chooses one or more of the order and delivery options. Because item-level RFID dramatically improves inventory accuracy, it will be a key enabler of omnichannel commerce.

Before I jump into all that, though, let me first say that technology by itself isn't a cure-all. There is plenty of software being touted as the solution to every supply chain issue. But to my mind, what leads to the big ROI is how technology is chosen, implemented, and used every day by knowledgeable, creative, educated, trained, and dedicated people. This was something I think the Integrated Logistics team at Nabisco demonstrated day in and day out, and it is one of the main points I tried to make in Chapter 6.

A major barrier to successful implementation of any technology is overcoming the resistance of senior management to fund a proposed project. We've been seeing a lot of this as companies have resisted investing in technology since the fiscal problems and the recession hit the USA. Education is the key: You have to educate senior management, and then the rest of the organization, with the support of senior management. This has to happen with an emphasis on how the new technology will impact departments, their service providers, customers, and consumers. Each of them has to be aware of and understand the new approach to managing the business.

Let's move on.

A Brief Introduction to ILRFID

RFID—radio frequency identification—is a technology that uses radio waves to transmit an item's unique identifying information, such as a serial number, or product and shipping information, from a tag to a reader. The reader takes that information and sends it to a computer system. (I won't be able to go into great detail on this complex s ubject here; for more information, I highly recommend *RFID Journal* (www.rfidjournal.com), including its magazine, website, and educational events.)

ILRFID involves tagging and tracking individual items such as apparel or other products in the retail supply chain. This technology can help address and overcome some of the common problems associated with inaccurate inventory information that retailers continue to struggle with today, as they have since consumers began shopping at retail outlets. To understand how it does so, it helps to first understand what those problems are. So here we go.

The current system of inventory control has a history of errors at every touch point, and at each of those touch points, there is a cost associated with the error. On top of that, the current methods of capturing product information provide marginal accuracy. For example, reading the bar code with a scanner requires line of sight and being within 9–12 inches. Given this circumstance, physical inventories take a long time and are very costly. Consequently, most companies will take a physical inventory once or twice a year, at their distribution center and in their stores, most often using an outside contractor. Some companies use cycle counting, which means they inventory product groups at different times of the year, hoping this will solve their problem. And this could be true, but there are a lot of conditions to be considered; for example, the number of products, importance of date codes, and the number of manufacturing and distribution points.

Typically, when a physical inventory is about to be taken, the accuracy of the product inventory—which takes into consideration the size, color, and style of a stock-keeping unit (SKU)—is in the range of 65 percent to 70 percent. The inventory count is somewhat accurate after a physical; however, accuracy declines at a rate of 2–3 percent per month. So it is understandable that at the end of a season or sales cycle, markdowns are prevalent; they are an attempt to sell product that didn't move during the season.

Among the typical reasons why that happens is that the product is in the wrong store because the forecast was seriously in error, or the product was hidden in the storage area of the store and not brought out to the sales floor, or if it was on the sales floor, it was on the wrong rack or rounder and was not noticed by the sales clerks. As a result, it was missed by the consumer. From a practical standpoint, just walk the garment floor of a retailer and ask yourself, "How difficult is it to find a particular garment if it is on the wrong rack?" I just went through this experience myself at a retail store. I enlisted the sales associate to help me find the garment I was looking for that frustrating afternoon. Well, she checked her inventory report, and the product was shown as being available, but it was nowhere to be found. She promised to follow up, find the garment, and call me. It's now three weeks later, and the call never came! The purchase was never made.

Forecasting software will make adjustments, given the expectation of errors, and apply algorithms and triple exponential smoothing (a statistical analysis method that captures important data patterns over a period of time). To account for the expected forecasting errors, inventory management systems will provide safety stock, typically in the 2–3 week range.

The major message to be gained from the scenarios outlined above is that incorrect inventory information results in a substantial amount of extra effort, cost, and lost sales! When the product isn't available when the consumer is ready to buy, it causes numerous problems in terms of consumer confidence. The damage done to consumer confidence is exacerbated when the product is on promotion and not on the sales floor! And just imagine the damage to the reputation of the store if the inventory information is incorrect and the product is ultimately found and moved to retail, but too late—the consumer has discovered the same item on sale at a competitor's store and buys it there.

These problems can be avoided with item-level RFID. ILRFID is a "magic wand" that can read tagged product even when it is inside a case!

Here's an example. We have successfully used a process called the electronic proof of delivery. Here's the way it works. The supplier packs out a case of product—let's say several pairs of socks, a few T-shirts, and for good measure, a few boxer shorts. The supplier prepares a packing slip identifying the customer and contents of the carton. The supplier electronically "reads" the contents of the case to ensure there is agreement with the packing slip. The information from each case that is packed and read is used to complete an Advance Ship Notice (ASN), which is transmitted to the retailer. When the order is received by the retailer, the case is read again, and it's highly probable that there is agreement in the 99.8 percent range.

Typically today, using the bar-code system, the retailer will pull up to 10 percent of the cases off the receiving line to check them. If there is an inaccuracy, e.g., the ASN and the case contents are not in agreement, then the retailer will short-pay the invoice and complete reconciliation when the next inventory is completed.

Now, suppose that item-level RFID had been employed in the example above. Imagine the productivity that could be realized on the receiving floor, the rapidity of turning the door and truck around, the ability to read each individual item inside the case, and the beat goes on. Imagine how, with ILRFID, a retailer could run product off an inbound truck and directly to an outbound carrier destined for a store. It's about customer satisfaction, solid retailer and seller relationships, and streamlined supply chain operations. Hey, call that productivity personified. One can easily come to the conclusion that every touch point can be positively affected by the use of ILRFID.

I'd like to take a moment to bring in the concept of Electronic Product Code (EPC)-enabled ILRFID—the nirvana that industry has been seeking since the advent of the bar code. My friends at GS1 US, the standards organization that now encompasses VICS, have done a lot of work in this area. Here's how they describe it on the group's website:

The use of the Electronic Product Code (EPC) with RFID provides an effective bridge from today's barcode-based systems to RFID without losing your current investment in identification systems, transaction systems, or other information sharing techniques. EPC-enabled RFID, coupled with serialization techniques, represent a way for your company to extend your current investment in the GS1 Standards to take advantage of the benefits of RFID as a data capture technology, while still using the GS1 standards for identification and data exchange.

We are almost there and will definitely see this great technology increasing by leaps and bounds in the very near future. (You can read more about this subject at www.gs1us.org. Patrick Javick, vice president of retail apparel and general merchandise, has also written articles for various industry publications about EPC-enabled ILRFID.)

Item-Level RFID Moves Forward

We'll talk more about the benefits of this technology later in the chapter, but I think it's important to share the path I traveled in becoming a zealot of item-level RFID.

My first hands-on experience with ILRFID was when I was with VICS and visited El Puerto de Liverpool in Mexico City in 2007. Liverpool is a Mexico-based department store chain that at that time had 78 stores with annual sales of US $3 billion. The previous year, the retailer had launched a comprehensive RFID solution for its 200 suppliers to help improve its inventory management processes. Liverpool's goal was to increase merchandise availability to near-perfect levels.

I was thoroughly impressed with how Liverpool had Levi Strauss & Co. source-tag jeans, and with how jewelry and eyeglasses were item-tagged in the retailer's distribution center. I was especially impressed with the jewelry that was in open-front displays, which allowed the shopper to inspect the product without a sales clerk present! This was also true for expensive eyeglasses. Security was ensured because a store clerk had to deactivate the tag before merchandise could leave the store; otherwise, an alarm would sound. Consequently, shrinkage was almost nonexistent.

Levi's source-tagging led to a smoothly operating supply chain. It allowed for the replenishment of product based on consumer purchases, with a relatively short turnaround time. This was a major factor in ensuring that product was available to meet consumer demand. (Today Liverpool's sales exceed US $4 billion across 85 stores, and the company continues to pursue its goal while expanding the use of item-level RFID to other product categories.)

I found myself intrigued by item-level RFID, and followed up with a conversation with Bill Hardgrave, director of the University of Arkansas (UARK) Walton College RFID Research Center. We discussed how VICS and the university could work together to support the use of ILRFID, starting with item-level tagging for apparel/footwear. I also contacted Mark Roberti, owner and editor of *RFID Journal*. He shared the history of RFID and how the concept was first developed during World War II to identify aircraft, and he explained how commercial applications expanded following work done by the Massachusetts Institute of Technology's Auto-ID Lab. This helped me understand the development of this technology and the credible organizations that had been involved for a number of years. (You can read his fascinating article on the history of RFID online at www.rfidjournal.com/articles/view?1338.)

Early on, RFID was mostly used on cases and pallets for tracking purposes. Wal-Mart Stores was among the first to do this, mandating that some of its suppliers use RFID. Although this was a thought-leading idea, the value was not there for the suppliers, and that first initiative did not really take hold. Nevertheless, the technology did work! Walmart's experience reinforces the idea that RFID has to be a collaborative initiative, with both the retailer and the supplier realizing benefits.

But people had been thinking about item-level RFID for quite a few years. In 2007, Bill Hardgrave, David Cromhout, and Justin Patton conducted research on why retail was slow to adopt item-level RFID. Not long after that, VICS and UARK established a partnership with the aim of launching some test pilots for the application of ILRFID in retail. We made such significant progress that in June 2008 Prof. Hardgrave presented at the VICS annual conference, and the first of five annual RFID Forums (2008 through 2012) was held at the UARK RFID Research Center. Justin Patton and David Cromhout did outstanding work in organizing the forums and helping with all the arrangements, which covered every imaginable function of a distribution center and a retail sales floor where you could use RFID technology.

Meanwhile, the UARK RFID Research Center in 2007 had partnered with Dillard's, J.C. Penney Co., and Macy's-Bloomingdale's to study improvements in inventory accuracy through item-level RFID tagging. The retailers agreed to conduct two-year pilots in collaboration with the Research Center team and several technology providers.

The Dillard's pilot showed consistent inventory-accuracy improvements thanks to item-level tagging, with the results published in April 2009; the Macy's/Bloomingdale's results, published in August 2009, showed improved inventory accuracy and reduced shrinkage; and the J.C. Penney study showed improved inventory accuracy, with the results published in April 2010. A big surprise was that each retailer also achieved an increase in sales because in-stock rates were higher. (The results of the pilots, as well as reports on UARK's research on applications for apparel, pharmaceuticals, and other industry segments, can be found at http://rfid.uark.edu/research-papers.asp.)

Despite those stellar results, it was still necessary to "sell" the ILRFID mission to the retailers' top executives. In mid-2009, I had the pleasure of attending the presentation on that subject that was made to the Macy's executive team in Secaucus, N.J. I was keenly aware of Macy's management's commitment to the use of the bar code and electronic data interchange (EDI) as the foundation of their very successful supply chain management processes and their relationship with their suppliers. I just wasn't sure how the presentation would be received, and I was not alone in this regard.

At the conclusion of a very objective and candid presentation made by Roger Blazek, the executive in charge of the Bloomingdale's pilot—with the highlight being a 6-percent sales lift on the products included in the pilot—I took a deep breath as a hush fell over the room. After what felt like a very long time, Tom Cole, the senior executive involved in the program, asked his team, "Where do we go from here?" I darn near jumped out of my chair and applauded. You see Tom Cole is one of the most knowledgeable, end-to-end supply chain executives in the retail industry, and his ideas are very influential. This essentially was the approval to move forward with developing a business plan for companywide implementation. It was followed by a presentation to the Macy's board of directors, which in turn led to the approval of the necessary capital for a permanent project, thus enabling Macy's/Bloomingdale's to embrace item-level RFID! By mid-2013 Macy's-Bloomingdale's had made good on its pledge to implement this technology at all 850 of its stores, and the company continues to expand ILRFID to more products and functions.

There is little doubt that the success of these pilots spring-boarded item-level RFID into global prominence, creating substantial interest due to the fact that each of the retailers realized an increase in sales. The most significant interest and activity has been in the apparel category, with 19 of the top 30 apparel retailers investing in or deploying RFID, according to Bill Hardgrave, who is now dean of the College of Business at Auburn University.

To help move the adoption of ILRFID forward, in 2010, representatives of retailers, suppliers, technology companies, educators, and industry associations (including the Council of Supply Chain Management Professionals, under the leadership of Rick Blasgen, who has always been a strong supporter of ILRFID) got together at a VICS meeting in San Antonio and decided to launch the VICS Item-Level RFID Initiative (VILRI).

The group describes its purpose this way:

... to develop collaborative and measurable value propositions for retailers, suppliers, consumers and other stakeholders, and to continue to develop business applications and best practices around standards-based RFID that demonstrate the impact of EPC-enabled RFID technology on processes and products within the global supply chain. We want to define a strategy for the phased introduction of item-level RFID technology into the supply chain whenever appropriate.

VILRI was led by Bill Connell, a retail executive from Macy's, and Cindy DiPietrantonio, an executive from the supplier Jones Apparel. These two very experienced supply chain professionals brought great value to VILRI. It also had an advisory board, with five subcommittees and several working groups. We recognized the value that technology providers would bring, so they were also included. The group had very broad support and participation by subject-matter experts who contributed to a number of meaningful programs that gave ILRFD broad visibility. This was a perfect example of a collaborative initiative designed to develop the path to successful implementation.

By the middle of 2011, VILRI's membership exceeded 200 individuals and 75 companies. In September of that year we launched the VILRI.org website with help from Mark Roberti of *RFID Journal.* By March of 2012, membership had grown to more than 250 individuals and 90 companies—and we hadn't even publicly announced the initiative yet! In November 2012, we formally launched VILRI with a press release "Retailers and Manufacturers Announce Joint Effort to Advance Use of Item Level RFID." We were very fortunate to have Mark provide his support and experience to VILRI.

It was an exciting time, and I had the pleasure of collaborating with a number of subject-matter experts, including retailers, suppliers, academics, trade associations, GS1 US, and technology providers. VILRI made amazing progress in a relatively short period of time. One of the most successful of our initiatives was the Solution Provider Sponsorship Program (SPSP). There were three levels of participation, which provided us with the funding to conduct webinars that were moderated by Mark Roberti. We published a newsletter edited by Mark and held nine industry dinners for retailers, suppliers, and SPSP members across the country.

During these informal dinners the invitees shared their experiences with ILRFID and learned from one another. Sometimes their views were very different. I recall one interesting exchange where a retailer with some 4,000 small stores said that she couldn't see the value of the technology. She was followed by another retailer with thousands of stores across the country, who shared the dramatic improvements his company realized in its logistics operations, sales, and customer service as a result of ILRFID. I think these informal discussions and opportunities to share experiences were instrumental in convincing executives of the value to be gained from implementing ILRFID.

The VILRI team delivered numerous presentations, conducted more than 50 media interviews and 10 analyst briefings, and appeared in 40 articles in 30 different publications. There was no doubt that we had earned the interest of the retail industry, as we provided very objective and candid information. I am so very proud of our team and what we were able to accomplish with limited resources. It points out what can be realized when there is a commitment to excellence and, just as important, the willingness and ability to collaborate with multiple partners. However, it does point out that it takes a village—and leadership!

This important, collaborative effort continues today, under the auspices of GS1 US. You can learn more about the initiative, the benefits of item-level RFID, and new developments in the technology at www.vilri.org.

By the way, VILRI was very supportive of EPCglobal (www.gs1.org/epcglobal), an organization that focuses on the development and use of Electronic Product Code (EPC) and RFID standards.

What Can ILRFID Do For You?

Let's pause here to review in more detail some of the benefits most companies should be able to achieve by implementing ILRFID. Developing this information was a joint effort among UARK, the VICS Item-Level RFID Initiative (VILRI) committee, and technology providers. It's reprinted here with the kind permission of *Retail TouchPoints,* an electronic publication for retail executives. It originally appeared in "VICS Item-Level RFID Initiative Leads Charge to Retailing's Future," an article I contributed in March 2012.

> **Reducing out-of-stocks** — This is more critical than ever, not only for apparel, but in all product groups. Keeping store inventory to an absolute minimum is critical to success. Sacrificing efficiency in order to meet consumer expectations—and vice versa—is no longer an option. Today's highly competitive marketplace dictates that companies must do both to be successful.

> **Increasing sales and increasing store and supply chain productivity** — This will certainly make a contribution to the retailer's and the supplier's bottom line. Pilots have indicated that having the right mix of products that consumers want to buy will maximize sales, maintain adequate shelf availability, and help keep prices competitive.

> **Lowering the cost of inventory** — Avoiding out-of-stocks and markdowns is very important, but the limited selling seasons of apparel and the frequent reconfiguration of products on the sales floor makes this challenge very difficult without item-level RFID.

127

Improvement of speed to market — With many products, trends and consumer preferences emerge rapidly, especially in the fashion business. Products have to get from design to the store faster than ever, sell, and be replenished as quickly as possible, while consumer interest is at its highest and before the next selling season begins.

Reducing labor — Retailers routinely slash prices to move merchandise, which results in lower gross margins. Improving store-level inventory accuracy and the number of SKUs that can be read with item-level RFID vs. the bar code reduces labor for taking inventory and searching for products. As source tagging is broadly implemented, retail and manufacturer labor productivity will improve. The supplier will also have fewer order discrepancies to resolve along with order status.

Generating data to maximize programs — The marketplace is rapidly embracing marketing programs with a goal of driving store traffic. Retailers need accurate, real-time information to determine what promotions are working and which ones aren't. Suppliers need this information to determine which marketing campaigns they will continue to fund. Retailer promotional programs represent about 25% of sales, so the impact can be substantial.

Preserving brand integrity — Counterfeiting is a significant problem, estimated to be at $1 trillion worldwide. It erodes brands and margins, and it causes confusion in the marketplace. Consumers don't know if they are buying legitimate, branded products. Item-level RFID, with GS1 US EPC-enabled serialization, is the one approach that can comprehensively address this challenge.

Consumer satisfaction — Harvard Business School research has consistently found that when a product is out of stock, the interested customer is highly unlikely to return to that outlet, and will shop for the product in another store. Research by the University of Arkansas found that the retailers participating in item-level RFID pilots each saw an increase in sales as a result of having product in stock (about 6 percent).

Reducing shrink — The overall average for retail shrink is 1.45 percent of sales. The average in apparel is 1.87 percent, computer and electronics is 0.97 percent, cosmetics and perfume are 1.79 percent, jewelry is 1.06 percent, shoes is 0.85 percent, and vehicle parts is 1.77 percent. There is a major opportunity to reduce shrink, including customer and employee theft, with item-level RFID.

Numerous studies by academic researchers and consulting firms have confirmed and continue to confirm the value of ILRFID. For example, according to *Item-Level RFID Tagging and the Intelligent Apparel Supply Chain,* a white paper from Motorola Solutions, companies that have implemented item-level tagging are achieving inventory accuracy rates of 98–99.99 percent and have seen sales jump by 4 percent to as much as 21 percent.

That echoes the findings of research conducted by the University of Arkansas and sponsored by GS1 US and the American Apparel and Footwear Association. The purpose of the research was to detail the value of EPC-enabled item-level RFID in supplier operations. The report compared item-level RFID to manual audits. Here are just a few of the researchers' conclusions:

- Although inventory accuracy in manual audits was high, it required a large sample—sometimes as much as an entire batch—to be confident of the level of accuracy.
- Even when volume is increasing, RFID can keep pace with 100 percent of tagged inventory. Manual audits cannot always do that.
- RFID-based audits experienced an error rate of only 0.01 percent. Manual audits had error rates of between 1 and 5 percent.
- RFID/EPC audits are more cost-effective because they do not incur the kind of additional labor costs per item that a manual audit does.
- Claims costs when implementing RFID audits were a fraction of those incurred using manual audits.

Despite all the successes and the good work being done to promote item-level RFID, the retail industry does not seem to be giving as much attention to it as maybe it should. In early 2013, I made a presentation and participated in a discussion forum at a retail conference that focused on supply chain management. While there, I spoke with about 30 executives about ILRFID, and about half asked for more information, which I gladly provided. But the conference itself did not include any sessions covering ILRFID! This was puzzling to me, since the need for more timely and accurate item-level information in retail is greater than ever.

Where Do We Go Now?

Up until now, the majority of the ILRFID implementations have involved apparel, footwear, and the like. But I think the number of applications will grow.

Grocery, the industry where I spent most of my career, may ultimately benefit from item-level RFID as the technology develops and the pricing of individual items is no longer an impediment. However, there is no reason why item-level RFID can't be used in the logistics side of grocery. Dreamers can make it happen, but keep in mind, it will require collaboration.

Item-level RFID could get its biggest boost from the rapidly growing interest in omnichannel merchandising. There are aspects of omnichannel merchandising that will make it one of the most complex business processes that retail has ever experienced. The only system that can deliver accurate product information is item-level RFID. Unless the retailer makes ILRFID a priority omnichannel will not deliver on its full potential.

Consider the sheer complexity of serving and meeting the expectations of omnichannel consumers. They are encouraged to purchase products online, at the store, via mobile device, or any other method supported by the retailer. They expect to have that product delivered to any destination they request, on time and exactly as ordered. They can buy online and pick up at a store, or buy online and have it delivered to their home or office, and if a product isn't available at the store it will be shipped to the consumer from another store location, a company replenishment point, or a supplier.

Now let's consider the complexity and uncertainty that will be created. Retailers that are involved in omnichannel may use multiple stores as replenishment points in addition to distribution centers. Macy's, for example, was filling orders from nearly 300 of its stores by the middle of 2013, and has said it plans to have as many as 800 stores act as replenishment points, with ILRFID as the critical enabler. Now the question is, how does the retailer plan for replenishment of those stores? That will be a major challenge, as it will be difficult to establish shipment profiles on one hand and in-store demand on the other. Then there is the issue of forecasting for replenishment by the supplier, and whether the supplier will be responsible for shipping to a consolidation center or directly to the stores.

You can easily see that the complexity that is building with omnichannel fulfillment will have an impact on the training and education of store personnel. Their roles will be far more challenging than they are for the conventional store associate, and they will have to develop an understanding of supply chain management.

If omnichannel is going to meet consumers' expectations, the entire retail system has to take steps to improve inventory accuracy. The methods used today to take physical inventories are simply not accurate enough to support fulfillment from so many locations. The typical product inventory is 50 percent accurate after six months; accuracy deterioration begins right after a physical inventory is taken, and it continues until the next physical inventory. Inaccurate inventory combined with varying demand in retailers' omnichannel system combines to make accurate forecasting a major challenge for the retailer, which in turn affects the replenishment program on the supplier side of the business. There is no doubt in my mind that item-level RFID is the only technology that is capable of ensuring the level of inventory accuracy that omnichannel commerce demands.

I think ILRFID can be viewed as a "disruptive technology"—one that will fundamentally change the way business is conducted. I hope you will agree that we have made a strong case for item-level RFID as a technology that provides many benefits and is key to gaining visibility of timely and accurate information on the location and quantity of a product, and, in some cases, even the quality of temperature-controlled products.

This is information that will make the use and role of distribution resource planning (DRP), manufacturing resource planning (MRP), sales and operations planning (S&OP), forecasting, supply chain operations (including shipping and receiving, efficient distribution center operations, transportation, store shrink, reducing unsaleables, reducing markdowns, selling more product at full retail—really, every aspect of business management—more relevant to the success of every business, regardless of product offering.

There continue to be barriers to implementation: tight budgets for spending on technology, the lack of trust between trading partners and solutions vendors, and the inaccurate assumption that only big retail chains can afford and benefit from ILRFID. But I feel confident that this technology will be such a game-changer in terms of cost, accuracy, and efficiency that at some point in the future, adopting item-level RFID will be considered a no-brainer.

I'm not selling ILRFID software, hardware, tags, or consulting. I'm totally objective and I want to see our retail industry become the model for the world to follow.

Chapter 8: Bringing It All Together

The journey that has been laid out in this book encompassed every business experience imaginable. As I wrote each sentence, my mind was flooded with so many memories, some that brought a smile to my face, others that unsettled my stomach, and still others that raised the question: "How did our team accomplish as much as it did during so much turmoil?" Two colleagues I respect suggested during a discussion about the book that the answer is that we worked with such great people! I totally agree—people with a team mindset overcoming many of the obstacles that were placed in their path are what made the difference.

What still amazes me is that our team hung together during the good times and bad. There was a bond that formed between our friends and associates that still exists today! At a recent Nabisco Alumni meeting, several of the attendees commented that they have not worked for any organization that they respected and enjoyed as much as they did during their time with Nabisco Brands. All of them have moved on to other positions and are making contributions to their present employers, using much of what they learned at Nabisco.

We had all worried about so many things—would our company be spun off entirely, or would it be done by brand, leaving us without a job? In addition, there were so many changes taking place that no company had experienced, including the largest leveraged buyout in history. While all this was going on, I questioned whether I would be willing to stay on even if it meant spending more years in uncertainty. After reflection, my answer was that I would opt to stay with our team and not jump ship since they depended on me, or at least that is what I told myself!

I also think that each setback actually made me stronger as I rallied my internal resources, stood up to the test, and came out on top. This was so important to my self-esteem. There's an old saying in Latin, "*Illegitimi non carborundum*." In English it expresses the great attitude of never letting the (expletive) get you down. Sure, we all had our ups and downs, but we enjoyed the "ups" and thought of them as building blocks. The "downs" identified what we could fix, and if they had to do with political decisions, we put them in perspective and moved on.

A Case of Déjà Vu

The following short vignette will help put into perspective what was happening on the ground as a result of the many changes that took place at Nabisco.

There used to be an annual off-site management meeting that consisted of a day of presentations, followed by cocktails and dinner. One year we met in Scottsdale, Ariz., at a popular hotel that had five locations, each with the exact same design. After dinner one evening I was asked to spend time with an executive, in his room, to discuss a very important business matter. As we sat down, the executive placed a folder on the coffee table that sat between his chair and mine. He then began to tell me that the organization appreciated the contribution I had made and the commitment I had shown. He then went on to say that I was viewed as "apple pie, motherhood, and the American flag," and then basically told me that I just didn't fit! I was more than shocked because this came right out of the blue. I just wanted to get out of there as soon as possible; I recall saying that if the company wanted me to leave, then I would have to be terminated for cause. Can you imagine the reaction of the business community if I were terminated for not fitting into the culture of the company?

It just didn't make sense. I, the director responsible for all of Nabisco Foods' logistics operations—the very foundation of the organization—was being summarily discharged because I was the essence of apple pie, motherhood, and the American flag. How should anyone handle a counterintuitive decision like this by management/HR?

134

I left the room and called my wife, Regina, completely overwhelmed. She counseled me to put it out of my mind and relax as best I could. Most importantly, she advised that I not pursue the subject with anyone, and let management take any next steps.

My own internal strength, plus knowing full well that the goals of the organization were being met—in fact, exceeded—did a lot to calm me down. But as we all know, we can't entirely separate our personal lives from our business lives. This type of trauma can have many negative consequences.

One week followed another, and then month followed month. There was not another word said to me about leaving the company. With each week that went by the uneasiness decreased. I focused on the job at hand and refused to let what I considered to be irresponsible actions lessen my belief in myself as a professional or as a husband and father. I think that having the opportunity to overcome many similar obstacles in my lifetime allowed me to have the intestinal fortitude to fight off this negative experience.

Flip the calendar forward one year, to another annual meeting with the same team in Scottsdale, at the same hotel chain but a different location. On the third day, there was a western-themed barbeque, with plenty of good food, refreshments, and a lot of conversation. At one point, I noticed a small group of the senior management team engaged in conversation. It gave me an uncomfortable feeling given what had happened the prior year. Unbelievably, I was asked again to step up to the room of one of the senior leaders. It was like "déjà vu all over again," to quote Yogi Berra! I can still recall the setting and how we faced each other, separated by the coffee table. The room had exactly the same layout and décor as the room where we met a year before. My mind whirled with memories of our last meeting in Scottsdale. How could this be happening again?

This time, the executive told me that he had bad news that he wanted to share with me. He said he had just met with the head of HR and that he was told that he was being terminated. WOW. I was shocked, and could never have imagined this scenario playing out. There was some subsequent conversation about old times, and then I excused myself. As I walked down the hall, befuddled, I ran into a colleague and friend and gave him a brief overview of what had just taken place. We found a quiet bar and had a couple of drinks that helped calm me down. I just couldn't believe the turn of events. I got back to my room and called Regina. She wasn't anywhere near as shocked as I was and said that I likely had a silent supporter in the head office. There was no other practical reason for what had taken place and the subsequent impact on my career.

This was but one example of the kind of shenanigans that took place. Let me share two other examples that rattled my timbers.

One time, I was asked to prepare a budget that would be presented to management. It resulted in a number of questions about head count. I went back to work on the numbers and came up with a marginally higher head count. My superior told me not to highlight this change, as it wouldn't be noticed during the subsequent management presentation. During that presentation, the executive immediately picked up on the difference in head count and said that he should immediately terminate me for not being honest and highlighting the difference. With that, his finance person jumped in and said that he was aware of the changes and that I had not tried to obfuscate the facts. Imagine that—an immediate conclusion that I should be terminated based on an assumption and not on the facts.

Well, I wasn't terminated, but the relationship we had from then on was strained, mostly because he didn't like the person I worked for and continued to stir up unrest. Thankfully, he ended up being moved to another division and was later replaced with another person who had no experience with matrix organizations. The effort to educate and develop a working relationship started all over again, as did some subsequent challenges and accusations that had a negative impact on the division's sales. Yet another effort to control Sales and Integrated Logistics came roaring back.

Making the quarterly sales numbers was all-important. One time I was directed to not invoice a number of orders that had been shipped before the end of the quarter, because we had exceeded our sales. This meant that I had to direct the regions to pull certain orders from the billing cycle, even though they had been shipped to the customer. During a routine audit that happened about the same time, the auditors came up with the disparity between shipments and billing. I was immediately questioned, and I quietly accepted the responsibility. I apprised the executive to make him aware of the circumstances and the potential consequences we were going to see (i.e., a negative auditing report). Well, that was where it ended. I was told it was a decision that *I* had made and which should result in my termination! For some reason I skated through, after being told that I should never do that again.

Focus on What's Important

I'm sharing these stories to explain the kinds of "landmines" that can be encountered during any career. It's not that anyone is evil or wrongfully minded; it's just that the culture and pressure cause people to act different ways in difficult circumstances. I know I acted as a professional and hold no animosity toward anyone, which follows the advice of many specialists: to let negativity go and embrace a positive mindset. I always believed in conducting myself with integrity and doing what is right.

One of my main reasons for writing this book is to help individuals prepare for and execute a successful supply chain management and logistics career plan. I hope, too, that the book will help senior management, marketing, sales, manufacturing, procurement, and finance professionals understand the value that supply chain management and logistics can bring to the company. This is also about helping individuals overcome adversity and the surprises that are sure to enter their world. Chances are, this type of information won't be found in educational programs or other books.

Based on my experiences, I've offered advice here and there throughout this book. Now, as I bring it all together and wrap up, I'd like to leave you with some additional thoughts. The first is that there are certain keys to success that cannot be ignored. I'd put education right at the top of that list. Then there is hard work and a commitment to doing what is right. Team building and helping others to be successful should be on anyone's list. So should the willingness to get a bloody nose! By that I mean finding what you're passionate about and fighting to realize its potential, getting slapped down time and time again but also going back time and time again. Fight for what you believe in!

Here are some other recommendations. They sum up what's most important for anyone who wants to succeed not just in business but also as a manager, a mentor, and a human being:

1.   People are number one! Give them the tools to be successful.
2.   Create a positive culture and engender a positive, can-do attitude.
3.   Ensure that management is trusted because of its actions and concern for people.
4.   Meet and/or exceed commitments, both financial and operational.
5.   Ensure that enabling technology is pursued and employed.

6. Treat everyone fairly, including third-party providers and company associates.
7. Be customer-friendly, meeting and/or exceeding customer requirements.

I recommend following all of these guidelines simultaneously.
It has been done, and you can do it, too, with the right attitude,
team members, and support from management.

The prize is out there for anyone to win, and knocking down obstacles
is great fun.

I welcome your comments and questions, and would be happy to
respond. You can contact me at
joe.andraski@collaborativeenergizer.com.

Best wishes for success,

Joe

Afterword: A Few Words of Advice

When you consider all the experiences I had throughout my career, at companies large and small, in times of turmoil and uncertainty, and under management that was sometime good and sometimes incompetent, I guess it's no surprise that I've learned a lot over the years about working with people and about what it takes to succeed. I've shared a lot of that knowledge with you throughout this book. But to make it easier for you to take advantage of what I hope will be useful advice, I've gathered some of my thoughts here in short, easy-to-read nuggets.

Two pieces of advice I heard years ago made a big impression on me. One was when I attended a presentation by the football coach and sportscaster Lou Holtz. I vividly recall how Lou closed. He said that when you aren't sure what to do, ask yourself, "What would Jesus do?" I also vividly remember this advice given by the consultant Aubrey Sanford at a team-building meeting we held in the mid '80s: "Always speak from your heart." These two bits of advice will help you find peace of mind, which lays the groundwork for a feeling of confidence and the ability to take on the most difficult challenges.

Ready? Here we go.

Ten Tips for Personal Success

Speaking my mind has worked for me and against me, so my advice in this regard is to pick your spots, but always defend your integrity by speaking about what is right and by not hurting anyone intentionally.

You can make a difference in spite of the obstacles that are placed before you. Whenever you are personally challenged in your ability to meet your obligations in regard to your responsibilities and the people you manage, you will earn something from those experiences, and those are the lessons that count.

There are times when it may be expedient to take the path of least resistance, but that may not be the right decision. Accommodating another individual or department by joining them in requesting management approval of something that has questionable value will not get you the respect you seek.

People want to work with management they respect, and that respect comes in several different packages. Earning the reputation of being a subject-matter expert is a sure path to developing a substantial amount of respect.

No textbook can tell you the right decisions to make when it comes to dealing with the political context for organizational changes. Reach back to your prior knowledge and experience, and then use that in combination with your gut feeling to come up with the best way to move forward. The best advice is to keep a level head in the face of adversity or opportunity, and remain calm and positive.

It's not important to extol the virtues of your proposal. Instead, think of it and promote it in terms of how it will financially benefit the company. That will get management's attention, I promise! Your proposal has to be realistic and achievable in the time frame laid out for completion. If there are any exaggerations in terms of a leap forward, your proposal will meet a sure and instant demise.

Keep the "keep it simple, son" (KISS) idea in mind. This is extremely important, because the effort to differentiate a company can easily create unusual and unnecessary system and process requirements. The end result is increased administrative and information system costs, with service failures added in for good measure.

There will be politics to contend with in large companies, and perhaps in small ones, too. How well you can read the tea leaves and react to your gut feelings will significantly impact your peace of mind. There will be politically-based changes that will affect you but you will have no ability to affect the outcome. Take the blow like a champ that you are, get up, and "do what Jesus would do."

We all have our ups and downs. Enjoy the "ups" and think of them as building blocks. Use the "downs" to identify what you can fix. If they have to do with political decisions, put them in perspective and move on.

Collaborating with academics who are on the cutting edge of supply chain thinking will benefit your company, yourself, and the educational institutions. For example, the time I spent working with forward-thinking academics like professors Don Bowersox, Bud LaLonde, John Coyle, and others fostered ideas that could be embedded in the strategic plans of retailers, suppliers, consultants, third parties, and technology providers.

15 Business Rules to Live By

Now, here are my "15 business rules to live by."

1. Build a network of friends and business associates. Isolating oneself will not provide the information resources that are necessary to be a successful manager. It takes time, effort, and effective networking. Become involved with professional associations, and volunteer to serve on committees and take on various leadership roles. Be sure to formally and informally encourage members of your organization to do likewise.

2. Be aware of your personal appearance and that of every member of your organization. How you present yourself extends a message to your organization, the internal departments with which you collaborate, your customers, and service providers. Attention to every detail provides your colleagues with confidence that you and your organization can be counted on to deliver on commitments, each time, all the time.

3. Impress upon your organization the importance of "pressure up." This means that management shouldn't lean on employees to fix problems that are outside of their purview. Instead, employees should know when and how to communicate up through the organization. This keeps management informed and ensures that surprises are kept to a minimum.

4. Develop metrics that are relevant to the success of the corporation and that senior management can easily relate to the corporate strategy.

5. Develop a culture of cooperation within your organization, with company departments, and most importantly, with customers and service providers.

6. Recognize individual and departmental performance based on meeting goals and objectives.

7. Treat every associate with respect. Help everyone to understand that every position adds value and contributes to the overall success of the company.

8. Be fair, but hold to your principles. This will build a solid relationship with all levels of your organization. There will be situations where a team member must be terminated or a service provider let go. Take the necessary action, but be sure to do it in a way that delivers the important message that you are tough but fair.

9. Understand that there will be times when you will be on the winning side and other times when you won't meet senior management's expectations. Sometimes an outstanding performance may be outweighed by political considerations. Know when to stay and fight the good fight, and when to move on to other opportunities.

10. Submit articles and papers to leading publications. Having your articles published will have a positive impact on how the industry views your knowledge and will raise your esteem in the eyes of your customers.

11. Develop a rock-solid relationship with the customers that represent 80 percent of your company's business.

12. Hold annual meetings for your department and your top service providers that are designed to strengthen relationships and collaboration.

13. Build strong relationships with your company's sales team, at every level. This should include offering a logistics training program that will help the sales department contribute to each customer's profitability through improved business practices.

14. Respond to all inquiries and requests completely and on time. If a response date can't be met, send a message to that effect and include a new date.
15. A high degree of organization and orderliness must become part of your organization's culture. Include this principle in operating guidelines for warehouse, transportation, and administrative operations. In the military this requirement to be neat, organized, and in alignment is referred to as "Dress Right Dress." Everyone in our department knew the term and exactly what it meant.

And finally ...

Love those who love you with a commitment and a passion. This will carry over to who you are in the profession that you choose to pursue.

Appendix

In the Appendix, I've gathered information that expands on some of the topics covered in the various chapters. I hope you'll find them to be both useful and interesting.

Much of the information in this section was contributed by friends and former colleagues, as well as by publishers of industry journals where I've contributed articles in the past. I'd like to thank each of them for their generous contributions and for their support.

1. Some Thoughts on Managing Change

This article was contributed by Prof. Lloyd Rinehart, Associate Professor of Marketing and Supply Chain Management in the College of Business Administration at the University of Tennessee, Knoxville.

Joe asked me to write this, based on a conversation we had about the challenges of initiating change in organizations in a wide range of applications. Change management is a hot topic in many business school programs. At a minimum, students will be exposed to a class session or two on the realities of corporate culture and how that culture opens up to change, or stifles it!

It is also important to recognize that this is not a NEW issue. "Change" is a constant in competitive organizations in our economy. For example, the "millennial" generation is embracing "sustainability" as one of their business mantras. Well, in reality, this is not a new issue. The young "boomer" generation of the 1960s and 1970s had similar environmental concerns: petroleum shortages, population growth, air pollution, etc. However, during that time period, the economy (and those who led it) could not figure out how to create "economic benefit" from the ideas. Economic benefit, in most cases is viewed as: How do I make a profit from this today?

In the 1990s, companies faced opposition to change as they tried to implement warehouse management systems. Over the past 20 years, we have seen the challenges that companies faced in implementing enterprise resource planning (ERP) systems. Some of the challenges companies face in these environments are the result of the willingness (or lack of willingness) of people to embrace the change.

Today, sustainability is "hot," and we (the business community and business academics) are beginning to see economic benefits due to established reductions in movement of inventory that is inefficient or not necessary. Therefore, very similar changes to those of the '60s and '70s are being embraced more by senior management today because we see economic benefits evolving from the initiatives.

However, what makes sense and what is realistic are two completely different things. The efforts to initiate further changes in the accomplishment of these social/economic goals are driven through current popular management applications of "collaboration" between parties. Unfortunately, the change in a competitively grounded economy occurs at a "snail's pace," not at the "speed of light." The reason for that is that first, we have to focus on our core business, and if there is time, then we can consider new ideas. Unfortunately, in today's world of "do more with less," there is NEVER time for the new ideas.

I believe part of the problem with initiating change in organizations is the collaborative/consensus-driven culture that has arisen throughout our society. Now ALL decisions must go through committees, subcommittees, and other groups for input. By the time ALL of the feedback is compiled, the issue's timeliness has passed, or those who thought it was important have given up and don't care anymore!

In a previous generation, managers had the self-confidence that they could make good decisions, and they made them! I believe that we have lost that ability today. That does not mean that managers should not seek input from others, but they should also know the difference between "right" and "wrong," and decide based on those feelings and senses. Let me offer an example based on a story that I heard, secondhand,

145

about Ken Monfort, chief executive of Monfort of Colorado, at one time the largest supplier of steaks to restaurants in the United States. Greeley, Co., used to be known as a "cow town" because of the aroma that emanated from the massive Monfort feed lot north of town. Greeley was about four miles to the south. The story goes that Monfort's board of directors considered moving the feed lot operations from its original location to another location further away from Greeley. At the end of the discussion, ALL of the board members agreed that the "economics" identified in the financial studies of the project did NOT justify the move, and they voted against the decision. Nevertheless, Mr. Monfort then made the decision to execute the move. It should be noted that not ALL of Mr. Monfort's decision was based on "social" gut feeling; he did consider that the local government had negatively adjusted potential tax incentives, which was one motivation for initiating the move. However, a drive today on US Route 34, 15 miles east of Greeley near the community of Kersey, indicates that he made the right decision ... especially if you talk to "old timers" in Greeley who will confirm that the town does not smell like it used to!

My point is that managers need to know the difference between "right" and "wrong" decision outcomes, and then make the "right" decisions and execute them. Unfortunately, we are seeing various industry sectors where it is obvious that managers do not know the difference between "right" and "wrong," and their decisions reflect that lack of decision-making skill.

Two things come from this discussion. One is that we have to change the mentality that ALL decisions must be made in an open consensus environment. However, companies must ensure that the managers in charge have the ability to make the "right" decision. That means that those managers must take the initiative and direct the organization. I don't like to call it dictatorial, but sometimes the only way to get things done is to look subordinates in the eye and say, "consider this a directive and do it!" Unfortunately, too many times people at the top of organizations assume that a general expression of interest in concepts and ideas will transcend into action at lower levels of the organization. Without what McGregor called "Theory X Management Control," many ideas get lost in the organization and never generate the benefits that could be derived.

This failure is due to a lack of understanding of the process that is being executed. That process, to varying degrees of success, is negotiation! Regardless of whether consensus is being pursued, a manager makes a decision for implementation, or a negotiation takes place, in the end

146

the outcome of the decision should be the execution of the action that evolved from that decision. However, if we look at these two strategies as end points on a continuum ...

Management Decision   Group Consensus

|---|

... we see that the closer the strategy is to an "authoritarian" management decision the more power the manager has in the organization. This reflects the decision-making and negotiation process used to move the initiative forward. (Remember, Mr. Monfort was CEO of a private company at the time!) However, the closer the strategy is to group consensus, the more the parties share power in the decision-making/negotiation process.

Personally, I don't care where organizations fall on this continuum. However, I do care that things get done, and I sense that there are too many managers out there who think that all of our economy is collaborative and consensus-driven, and that doing nothing (or maintaining the status quo) is a better option than making unilateral decisions based on their power position in the organization.

All managers must recognize that every decision is a negotiation, and if they fail to pursue the execution of initiatives that they expect subordinates will automatically carry out (when in reality they don't), then those managers are giving up the power in the decision-making/negotiation process as it relates to the initiative. Therefore, every manager must determine how much power he or she wants, and how much power should be delegated to subordinates and others if strategies are to be executed.

I hope these thoughts stimulate discussion (both pro and con) that may advance the quality of decision making in your organization.

Lloyd M. Rinehart, Ph.D.
Associate Professor of Marketing and Logistics
The University of Tennessee, Knoxville

2. How West Marine Moved Forward With CPFR®

This description of how West Marine brought its suppliers on board with CPFR® was contributed by my old friend, Larry Smith, and is reprinted with his permission. Larry was a longtime member of VICS and an enthusiastic supporter of CPFR®. His role in developing information about CPFR® and sharing it with other companies cannot be overstated. He took his role as the chair of the VICS CPFR Committee very seriously and managed the development of the new initiatives with aplomb and great dedication. Larry is a role model for all of us who believe in making major change happen and bringing significant value to their companies and the industry at large.

When West Marine (WM) decided to go down the path of CPFR® they started with 20 suppliers that represented a significant percentage of their business. Each company was invited to a meeting at the WM home office to hear firsthand the requirements that they were going to be asked to fulfill. WM ultimately included some 200 vendors in the program—not the typical 10 percent of suppliers that, at the time, some proposed should be included in a CPFR® program. A well thought-out program, *à la* West Marine, clearly demonstrates how critical mass can be achieved, whatever numbers of trading partners are involved. The information sharing that took place during the initial meeting can serve as a model for other companies.

The meeting was labeled a "Supply Chain Summit" for vendors planning success with West Marine. A Supply Chain Summit is a conference with a small group of key suppliers. WM used this format to jumpstart their integration program. This presentation was intended to help individual Category Management teams hold similar conferences individually with their team or with small groups of vendors.

Larry Smith, Senior Vice President for Merchandise Planning and Replenishment at West Marine, helped lead the session. Larry introduced the merchandise planners at West Marine, who are the people who build, approve, and manage orders. The main point of the presentation and the supply chain business meetings that were scheduled was for the group to understand how the separate organizations work and how they can work together more effectively to improve overall supply chain performance.

Each participant, working with their West Marine team, was tasked with developing and executing specific and actionable strategies to achieve measurable improvements in the supply chain performance for the coming season. The participants in this conference come from many disciplines. All of the participants were supply chain and logistics participants in some way, shape, or form. Whether someone authorizes a trading agreement, develops marketing plans that result in purchases, plans and forecasts, purchases, or manages transportation or distribution, their business is the supply chain. We all pay the bills by actually getting our products to the customer when he wants them. Without this, the best product, brand, or marketing plan in the world isn't worth much.

The goal was for the group to leave the conference having learned to look at their contribution to the supply chain in a new way. Successful supply chains involve multiple organizations that learn to work together to improve total supply chain performance. Fundamentally, their success depends upon the group's success as a supply chain.

Once the introduction was completed, the following agenda helped lead the conversation:

- Mission of Planning at West Marine
- What our customers care about
- Current performance metrics, future requirements
- Planners: your supply chain partner
- Supply chain focus on consumer purchases
- Win by building to a collaborative order forecast
- Benefit of collect freight
- EDI
- Next steps

Larry was interested in making sure the teams left the meeting knowing how to take what they learned from the presentation and the business meetings and made clear and measurable improvements in supply chain performance.

Planning
The mission of planning is to improve stock and inventory performance, and to optimize supply chain technology and processes. Planning requires people and systems. Larry Smith believed that the summit participants would discover, through their follow-up planning meetings, key opportunities to grow sales with West Marine while improving their profit ratios.

What do our customers care about? Not supply chains. WM customers do not care or even know about supply chains. They only see their retail experiences while making a purchase in stores, on the Internet, through a catalog, and through the commercial sales force. To WM customers, the supply chain is really a value chain: it's how WM, as a retailer and as a manufacturer, provides their customers the best in availability and convenience, as well as the best value and product assurance to satisfy their boating needs and exceed their expectations. To serve them well WM needs to understand their supply chain and add value. According to Larry, just as West Marine's marketing partnership is the best choice the vendor participants could make, WM also wanted them to understand that with West Marine they can build a supply chain to customers that offers the best value and maximizes their own sales and profits.

Current and Future Performance Metrics
For the two years prior to the summit, West Marine had substantially increased average inventories of products in their stores. In 2001, WM even substantially smoothed out the supply chain by maintaining more inventory in stores, earlier in the year. WM committed to its vendors that they would own more depth and safety stock, and they did. In-stock is a measure of product availability for their customers.

Unfortunately, the increased inventory investment in stores did not change the in-stock result. WM learned that their supply chain performance was just not adequate to support higher in-stocks and thus higher customer satisfaction. In-stocks in off-season months were 96 percent to 98 percent, but at the peak of the season it was a struggle to be better than 95 percent. Keeping in mind that industry studies indicate that retailers' average in-stocks are about 92 percent and that lost sales are about 7 percent.

For the retailer, about half of out-of-stocks are offset by alternative sales of other products on their shelves. But for the manufacturer, less than 2 percent of lost sales are recouped by purchases from the same manufacturer or brand. How could WM improve stock during the next year? WM and its vendors needed to work together to improve timely and complete shipping to provide better product availability and sales. At this conference, vendors would learn how much work the West Marine team had done to improve the forecasting of sales and orders, as well as to improve the pattern and composition of the orders sent to the vendors. Each vendor's West Marine team was going to make some specific recommendations to make order quantities or distribution quantities more effective. The most desired, fundamental process

150

change was for the vendors to work with WM in identifying and resolving supply constraints before they occurred.

At the time of the summit, WM had the following vendor shipping metrics in place:

Number of receipts per purchase order: 2.1
For the first half of 2001, WM averaged over two receipts per purchase order, and some vendors averaged much higher. In effect, this means that West Marine incurred substantially more receiving costs, vendors incurred substantially more shipping costs, and WM incurred substantially higher shipping costs than they would otherwise have had if they had fulfilled orders completely.

On-time fill percent, even if more than one receipt: 30 percent of ordered quantity
WM's average on-time fill percent, even with multiple receipts, was only 30%. Late shipping products caused WM to miss sales, even though the company maintained high safety stocks of vendor items. WM and its vendors needed to work together to improve shipping and optimize the flow of product through the distribution network.

After the summit, WM added more measures of performance. WM managed its order components to reduce costs, bought in pallets and truckloads wherever appropriate, and produced orders to vendors that optimized both of their logistics capacities. High-volume vendors received truckload orders, one purchase order to the truck. High-volume items could be purchased in pallet increments. WM estimated that their ordering process, based on customer purchases, could provide a sales or operating cost benefit of 2 percent.

West Marine essentially converted the way they built vendor orders and forecasts to be based directly on aggregated consumer purchase demand. Previously, orders to the distribution centers were separately forecasted based on historical warehouse shipments. Inventory analysts at West Marine spent a large portion of their time attempting to optimize distribution center-level forecasts, and they did not have good visibility to store overstocks or shortages. With these changes implemented, orders and forecasts were based on customer purchases and recognized store inventories, making them far more accurate. WM data indicated that order forecasts were not only better than the industry standard, but are greater than 90 percent accurate (versus industry at 75–85 percent).

WM tuned up its store replenishment system to make it more responsive to an individual store's seasonality and changing business needs. They refined their forecasts not only by item, but also by item/store. WM also set seasonal selling curves, called profiles, by product for 11 climate areas. The capstone to this process was setting service levels by store based on the importance of stock-keeping units (SKUs) to each store's customers for a given time of year. The ranking system evaluated each store's products by unit sales, dollar sales, and margin. WM built ranking by weighing each of those three components about equally, based on forecasts for the next 13 weeks.

After the changes, the Port Clinton, Michigan, store actually had different "A rank" items than the St. Petersburg, Florida, store. Promotions were included in the order forecast. All promotional events were planned out in the ordering and forecasting system, by store. As soon as the category managers selected items and projected their expected sales lifts, WM entered promotional plans into the replenishment system. End caps, floor stacks, and any other special presentations were also planned in the system and included in vendor order forecasts. All these plans helped avoid overstocks by taking into account the product already on hand. WM would normally finalize promotional plans 8 to 10 weeks in advance, and planned even earlier if vendors requested this information in their forecast. WM planned purchases to build up stocks in advance of the season in 2002—it had a plan to have the right product in the right place at the right time.

Internally, West Marine had made great progress in their collaboration between planning and replenishment, and logistics and distribution center operations. WM set up a weekly forecasting conference to agree on one forecast for sales, receipts, and shipping. One forecast! Staffing was based on sales and store order forecasts. There were fewer capacity constraints by making more intelligent orders and streamlining product flow into distribution centers. Store inventories were built early, after learning about the cost benefit. WM also increased efficiencies by shipping more case packs; as vendors worked with WM to provide more retail-appropriate packs, WM drove more sales.

West Marine's internal supply constraints were solved by collaborating on a consensus forecast and on efficiency opportunities. WM changed the role of the merchandise planner so that they were vendors' supply chain partners. Each of WM's planners supported an individual category manager and directed a replenishment analyst on store-level item forecasting. Each vendor was assigned a "logistics captain." Planners were also responsible for building and managing orders to vendors. The planner whose CM had the majority of their products was the designated "supply chain captain," giving vendors a single point of contact for supply chain issues.

As vendors received one consolidated purchase order by shipping point, WM wanted to make sure it was optimized to reduce vendor and WM supply chain costs. A frontline supply chain collaborator was assigned to support vendors. Each vendor needed an appropriate frontline supply chain collaborator to work with the planner on orders, forecasts, and supply chain opportunities. WM estimated that their commitment to giving vendors a clear supply chain collaborator provided a sales or cost benefit of 1 percent to vendors.

Since West Marine invested heavily in people and technology to allow for the generation of solid sales and order forecasts, it was really up to vendors to leverage this technology by working collaboratively with WM on the order forecast and by using it in their manufacturing planning.

WM needed to identify supply constraints before they occurred and make sure these were resolved before customers were affected. This requirement presumed that vendors were analyzing and managing to the WM forecast and sharing findings with their WM planner.

The premise was that shortages cost vendors and WM sales, overtime, and expediting expense. Overstocks also cost significantly more than the financial cost to carry. Together, the group could work to reduce them—and to improve the forecast and making sure that within each vendor all departments (marketing, production, and logistics) shared in a single consensus forecast. WM estimated that collaborating and building to the forecast provided a sales or operating cost benefit to vendors of 2 percent to 4 percent.

While many retailers were still on a "delivered price" basis—where the supplier arranges for, pays the freight, and builds transportation cost into the price—West Marine had a different view. Why collect freight? WM had several, compelling reasons to convince its vendors:

- In almost all cases, West Marine had lower freight rates to reduce supply chain costs. Moreover, vendors no longer had to manage the freight flow.

- WM could work with key less-than-truckload carriers to consolidate freight with other vendor shipments. Their key LTL carriers had standing appointments with WM warehouses that prioritize their deliveries. In the peak season, receiving docks can't be tied up with partial loads from miscellaneous carriers.
- Faster receipt and shipping drive sales.
- More reorders = more sales. Sales will drive reorders.
- WM estimated that collect freight shipping provided vendors a sales or operating cost savings ranging from 1 percent to 1.5 percent.

The use of electronic data interchange (EDI)—the computer-to-computer transfer of secure digital information—facilitated low-cost, accurate information sharing. Traditional approaches to EDI were not cost effective for West Marine and their vendor base, but developments in Web-based EDI transmissions made this a high benefit-to-cost proposition. Each vendor had significant potential labor cost savings in purchase order keying, invoice reconciliation, and the current daily effort to manually share information on shipping and backorders. The cost of integrating EDI with vendor systems was low. EDI would allow vendor partnerships clearer metrics and accountabilities. Everyone would know when and what was shipped as soon as it was shipped. Bar-coded cartons or pallets reduced receiving discrepancies, which would speed the flow of products. Invoice matching and payment would be faster and more accurate. Along with the National Marine Manufacturers Association (NMMA), WM selected SPS Commerce, a leading third-party provider in Web-based EDI, to help make this happen. WM estimated that vendors would see sales or operating cost savings in the area of 1.5 percent if they stepped up to EDI.

Summary
There are several aspects of the West Marine on-boarding and ongoing collaborative program that stand out. The willingness of WM to share information and to be very clear about the steps WM and its suppliers must take to collaborate and achieve success was groundbreaking.

The steps WM took to organize their functional areas were/are models for others who want to take down silos within their companies. Imagine a work area with key departments (e.g., transportation, inventory management, sales, marketing, finance) in the perimeter of the room. In the center of the work area there is a meeting table, where the team can easily swing their chairs around and have an impromptu meeting to discuss a problem or opportunity.

Then there are the informal and/or intrinsic benefits of team members rubbing shoulders, getting to know one another, trust one another, working toward a common goal. Even though each may have a direct-line reporting relationship, there is a bonding opportunity possible that overcomes whatever barriers can frequently occur when the lines of responsibility are diverse, with department management on different plans, due to any number of factors.

This approach is no doubt an important part of the WM collaborative initiative that has delivered proven results and should be considered by any company striving for excellence. Of course any strategy has to have a value proposition, or else why would it be embraced by senior leadership? WM projected several financial benefits, which are more than impressive and must be taken into consideration. Here's a quick recap:

- Planner, logistics partner: 1 percent
- POS-based orders: 2 percent
- Build-to-order forecast: 2–4 percent
- Collect freight: 1–1.5 percent
- EDI: 1.5 percent

Well, they must have been on target, because the program continues to have the support of the WM supplier community to this day! So we have a proven value proposition, leadership support, a management team that takes pride in always challenging "what's next," and a successful enterprise.

3. Multi-Vendor Consolidation

One industry practice that falls under the category of collaboration is multi-vendor freight consolidation. It's an idea that has been around for some time but has not gained widespread support, for reasons I explain below. (The recent and growing focus on sustainability is helping to raise interest in consolidation, but it still has a long way to go.) This section reviews some of the benefits of multi-vendor consolidation and includes two examples of pioneering, highly successful programs.

The Joint Industry ECR (Efficient Consumer Response) Consolidation Work Group, ECR Best Practices Operating Committee, and CSC Consulting published in 1996 a comprehensive report titled

Consolidation: Strategies to Maximize Efficiency and Minimize Cost.
The report explains the benefits of freight consolidation this way:

"The objective of consolidation is to maximize the advantages of
critical mass in an environment of smaller, more frequent shipments.
Successful consolidation requires a critical mass of suppliers to
ensure enough volume to consolidate orders on a daily basis. ...
This allows the suppliers to achieve the economies associated with
consolidating smaller, more frequent orders into truckloads while
maintaining required service levels. Concurrently, it eases the
anticipated dock congestion resulting from increased use of
continuous replenishment programs."

Initially, a number of companies (retailers, wholesalers, consultants,
sales brokers, suppliers, and public warehousing companies) expressed
interest and went forward with consolidation programs. The Grocery
Manufacturers Association (GMA), the Food Marketing Institute (FMI),
and a number of other associations held conferences on consolidation.
The conferences focused on case studies, metrics, implementation
guidelines, and reviews of the ECR document. The level of excitement
at the operating level was high, but the excitement didn't make it to
the executive level at the retailers or suppliers.

The ECR consolidation document was written by retailers, suppliers,
and entrepreneurs who built successful public warehousing companies.
It covers the consolidation process and defines benefits, requirements,
and performance measurements for implementing and managing
consolidation, case studies, and sample third-party capabilities
questionnaires.

We can draw a few conclusions. The committee that studied the
opportunity and wrote the document was made up of experienced and
knowledgeable individuals. The consolidation concept was supported
by leading retail associations (including the Uniform Code Council).
There was a very compelling business proposition (had sustainability
been in vogue back then, it would have been a very compelling reason),
and consolidation didn't require expensive technology or complex
business processes.

So the question is why hasn't it been more widely adopted in the
United States? The answer is straightforward: There were a number
of organizational silos within the retailer and supplier organizations.
Secondly, and equally important, there was a lack of trust among the

trading partners. There were concerns that one partner would realize greater advantages than another; consequently, the program would die off or never get off the ground as an accepted business practice. To be sure, there were and still are consolidation programs in place today, but they are nowhere close to mass implementation.

Let's review a couple of early examples of successful multi-vendor consolidation. Although these are not recent cases, they are exemplary and help to make the case for the future of collaboration.

Foxboro Distribution

Foxboro Distribution, located in Foxboro, Massachusetts, served the New England dry grocery and food service business for many years. (The company was sold many years after this story took place, and now operates under a different name.) Foxboro's CEO, David Petri, was one of the most forward-thinking individuals in the business and completely understood all aspects of handling and moving products effectively and efficiently. He also had a deep understanding of the retail supply chain. David, a hands-on executive who grew up in the business, came up with the concept of consolidation. Foxboro's clientele amounted to 60 suppliers, a sufficient base to support a consolidation program.

Quite a few years ago, David put in place the following requirements for consolidation to take place:

- Retailers and food service distributors were required to order in tier quantities, with a minimum of two tiers of each stock-keeping unit (SKU) per order. This improved warehouse productivity at both Foxboro as well as the retailer/food service distributor, as picking and putaway was efficient.
- By ordering in tier quantities, one and two SKUs included in an order were typically damaged or lost. This created the need to involve the accounts payable and receivable departments and a loss/damage claim. This is basically eliminated by tier ordering.
- All orders were picked by an assigned warehouse person who signed the pick ticket. If a problem occurred, it was easy to go to the responsible person and resolve the problem.
- Upon arrival at the destination distribution center, the trailer was assigned to a door with priority unloading. While most deliveries took five to six hours with conventional loads, the consolidation load took on average 45 minutes.

- Putaway at the destination distribution center was greatly facilitated by the tier/pallet loading, with putaway productivity gains in the 35 percent range.
- The retailer or food service company could order in smaller, more frequent orders. This reduced inventory carrying cost.
- Full truckloads were still being shipped as the retailer and food service company agreed to participate in the consolidation program. Orders were placed based on a profile maintained by the shipper as to the suppliers that were participating in the program.
- Fewer trucks shipped, reducing less-than-truckload (LTL) shipments. This would have been a real win today, considering concerns about sustainability and carbon emissions.

Keep in mind this was innovation at its best, with David and his team championing consolidation. David participated on the ECR Consolidation Committee, willingly offering his advice, experience, and counsel in the spirit of collaboration.

One last point: Because of the controls that the company put in place, deliveries were made to a warehouse club, where the product was received and entered into the inventory system without being counted!

It's no surprise that much of the information in the ECR consolidation document was contributed by David Petri.

ServiceCraft Distribution Systems
The second case study is about ServiceCraft Distribution Systems and its Shipping Consolidated Orders for Replenishment Efficiencies (SCORE) program. ServiceCraft was bought by Saddle Creek Logistics in 2009 and merged into Saddle Creek's system. However, because the events detailed below happened long before that, we'll use the ServiceCraft name here.

Some years ago, encouraged by Nabisco Foods, Tom Taylor and his team at ServiceCraft embraced the SCORE concept and enthusiastically took it to the grocers in their Los Angeles service area. The following are the SCORE program objectives:

- Consolidate all products from various manufacturers and deliver to retail or wholesale distributors in consolidated truckloads
- Unit-load ordering of manufacturers' products by distributor to allow a third party to build efficient, damage-free loads

158

- Eliminate silos of waste throughout the system
- Establish a strategic alliance that includes trust, integrity, shared vision, and goals
- Form effective partnerships with 29 manufacturers

The benefits realized by the retailers, manufacturers, and ServiceCraft were similar to those that Dave Petri's organization experienced. As an example of transportation savings, the LTL cost for four shipments of 10,000 pounds was $495. The SCORE program rate was $256.00. Here are some other numbers that show how quickly consolidation made a difference:

	2 Months Prior to SCORE	2 Months Post SCORE Implementation
Total shipped	714,408	695,103
Total loads	58	24*
Average weight per load	12,317	28,963**
Total orders	76	84
Average number of orders per load	1.3	3.5***
Overage, shortage, and damage	0	0

*59 percent reduction
**135 percent increase
***169 percent increase

Total inventory savings amounting to $1,792,105 were realized by retailers in the first six months that the program was offered. The number was sure to dramatically increase as more retailers participated. ServiceCraft rolled out the program to its Modesto, Calif., distribution center. That facility's business grew by 400 percent as retailers agreed to participate and encouraged manufacturers to place their products in Modesto.

Imagine if the grocery industry (including confections and other related products) had engaged in consolidation for the last 20 years for products typically shipped through grocers' distribution center networks. Imagine the substantial savings in transportation expense, inventory carrying cost, and more. If it had done so, the industry would have become a sustainability leader. This could have opened the way to other benefits, such as taking trucks off the road, causing less wear and tear on the highway and bridge infrastructure.

Consider how the retail industry has been moving to smaller orders, delivered more frequently. Major manufacturers that promote truckload, plant-direct pricing programs have pulled back. The retailers were not willing to carry the inventory or provide the additional distribution center space. The case is made for consolidation!

The family that used to own ServiceCraft moved its business to San Diego several years ago, and the consolidation program is alive, well, and growing under the States Logistics Services name. States Logistics has continued to learn, improve, and add significant value to the trade through its consolidation practices. The following is a more current example of the benefits of multi-vendor consolidation, contributed by W. Ryan Donovan, vice president of States Logistics Services Inc. (and a former Nabisco colleague). Here are the improvements the company and its clients have realized as a result of its consolidation strategy:

- Increased inventory turns (50 percent)
- Reduced inventory levels (45 percent)
- Improved on-time delivery (99.8 percent on time)
- Improved retail case fill (98 percent, improved for every manufacturer)
- Eliminated buyer/manufacturer delivery-date discrepancy
- Reduced shipping costs
- Reduced overage, shortage, and damage (OS&D); only eight OS&Ds in 7,980 shipments = .00100 percent
- Decreased administration costs and invoice discrepancies
- Scorecard improvement
- Preferred supplier status
- Reduced transit times
- Reduced carbon footprint
- Increased sales growth
- Increased productivity of operations
- Eliminated delivery sorting and segregating
- Diminished dock congestion
- Reduced average unload times from 5 hours to 1.21 hours

4. Commentaries

Over the years I've been invited to write columns for a number of industry publications. Because those columns touched on many of the same themes that are discussed throughout this book, I've included a couple of them here, with permission from the publisher.

I wrote the following column for the May 2012 issue of Fashion Mannuscript.

What Does It Take to Be Successful?
What can cows in China and elephants in Texas teach us about the future of apparel?

Several years ago I visited China. During one of my many stops I was treated to a tour of a very modern and successful dairy farm/producer. The owner was born and educated in California, and moved to China to fulfill his dream of being an entrepreneur. What was most surprising about the dairy was the fact that each of the 500 cows in the herd wore an RFID chip in their right ear and each of the portals the cows passed through was equipped with a reader, so the location of every cow was known at all times.

I was overwhelmed by the technology, and especially by the financial payback that was allowing the owner to grow the herd—with plans to go from 500 to 1,000 cows in a year—considering that he started with 100 head of cattle just a few years prior. Further reading revealed a zoo in Dallas, Texas, that was tagging elephants to be able to track the time spent in what part of the zoo and other relevant information. I could continue with a number of unique examples of how the RFID has been used to great advantage. The age of information has been with us for some time, but this technology has true game changing features.

There are numerous examples of companies that have implemented electronic product code (EPC) enabled RFID and which have enjoyed the benefits that serialization delivers. The VICS Item-level RFID Initiative (VILRI), for example, has been about developing operating guidelines and helping the trade understand the benefits of using information to meet or exceed consumer expectations. There are many companies out there that just don't understand the progress made over the last couple of years, so it is clear that education and communication are two of the keys to success.

VICS is a relatively small not-for-profit association that heavily relies upon its membership to lend their experience and expertise. VICS was created by several large department stores and mass merchants to address methods of improving efficiency and effectiveness. They agreed to employ the use of the UPC bar code, which tracked product from manufacturing through to store check out, improving inventory management and material handling.

From there, they embraced Electronic Data Interchange (EDI), which dramatically improved the accurate and timely movement of information. With the success realized, it moved on to logistics, floor ready merchandise, and several other initiatives delivering significant value to the entire busines process—from procurement to store management.

To determine the financial impact VICS initiatives could potentially make, Kurt Salmon Associates conducted a study:

- Identified $25 billion in industry cost due to supply chain inefficiencies.
- Quick Response (QR) was conceived as a business strategy for textile suppliers, apparel manufacturers, and retailers to remedy these inefficiencies through technology and collaboration.
- QR Revisited reviewed original business practice ROI and identified $13 billion of industry savings based on VICS supply chain practices.

It is obvious that this vision and the ability to execute helped establish VICS as an organization that could create value. The organization then went on to collaborate with GS1 US—back then the Uniform Code Council—in the use of the bar code and EDI, subsequently asking GS1 US to take up the management of VICS EDI. VICS and GS1 US now closely collaborate on the development of RFID technology employing GS1's Electronic Product Code (EPC) standard. This brings significant value to the progress that has been made, keeping in mind that GS1 US invested a substantial amount in the early days of RFID that was being used for cases and pallets.

Accenture conducted a survey of EPC Item-level RFID use among suppliers and retailers in North America in 2011:

- Retail supply chain wide rollouts by a number of North America's largest clothing retailers are a clear sign that this technology will be soon broadly adopted.
- Item-level RFID is becoming a competitive differentiator for several leading companies in retail.
- Costs for RFID tags and other technology are falling, while dramatic improvements are taking place.

GS1 and the American Apparel and Footwear Association sponsored research by the University of Arkansas, with the goal of detailing the value of EPC enabled item-level RFID in supplier operations. The report offers key findings when comparing item-level RFID to manual audit practices:

- Although an examination of manual audits demonstrated that inventory accuracy was high, the sample size needed to ensure confidence in that accuracy can be as large as an entire batch.
- RFID keeps pace with 100 percent of tagged inventory volumes even in times of volume increase, exceeding the capabilities of manual audits.
- When audited, RFID demonstrated a 0.01 percent error rate, compared with 1 percent and 5 percent error rates founds in manual audits.
- RFID/EPC audits present a lower and flatter marginal cost than manual audits by removing the upward shift associated with labor cost per item.
- Claims costs when implementing RFID were a fraction of costs incurred using manual audits.

The progress made by the industry would not be possible without the leadership of the Jones Group, Macy's, GS1 US, and VICS. The success of initiatives such as these will always be attributed to member commitment and willingness to contribute in so many ways. The baton was passed on several years ago—with the realization that new thinking is the key to success—to individuals with the ability to imagine what can be and then pursue a plan for VILRI and EPC enabled RIFD to provide the visibility necessary to improve sales and consumer satisfaction. The effort to provide education that will benefit the industry and to achieve broad scale implementation as soon as possible continues.

It's not too late for apparel companies, retailers, and technology providers to get involved in RFID initiatives.

I wrote this column for the November 2013 issue of Fashion Manuscript.

Leadership and the Realization of Supply Chain Collaboration

A successful company achieves a balance of a logical, orderly supply chain process on one hand and freewheeling entrepreneurship on the other. The ability to create an environment that stimulates such leadership at all levels of an organization will be the single greatest determinant of success in the new millennium. Logistics leaders will need to learn how to best deal with systems and human resources to achieve individual corporate and shareholder goals while simultaneously delighting customers. This will require a commitment to supply chain management and the collaboration necessary to facilitate cross-organizational cooperation.

The concept of supply chain management offers a way to fuse process and entrepreneurship. It is a truly holistic concept that begins with customers and integrates and focuses all effort from raw material procurement to finished product distribution.

Let's consider the future business environment, particularly for those publicly owned companies who will continue to be faced with Wall Street and shareholder demands for increased sales and profits. For the foreseeable future, consumers will demand more for less, demographics of population will continue to shift and inflation will remain a distant memory.

Given this scenario, why are companies resisting a process that is relatively inexpensive to implement, yet promising so much in terms of potential value? Several thoughts come to mind: turf, a lack of understanding by senior management, poor or nonexistent systems infrastructure, nonexistent change-management skills, and perhaps most of all, the absence of crisis. The answer can be found in any combination of the above. However, general resistance to change stands high as a SCM barrier.

It is a given that skepticism concerning the ability to forecast sales exists at every level. If supply chain management begins with a forecast that is substantially in error in terms of timing or quantity, the ramifications will be felt throughout the entire process.

So, the immediate push back of SCM is "without an accurate forecast, we are continually going to deal with an exception-driven business process." An opinion ventured—most companies are committing half of their resources to managing such exceptions, such as their sales, marketing and other operating and administrative groups. Such problem perception is a huge opportunity just waiting to be exploited.

Earlier, forecasting was a positioned as a prime culprit in the failure of supply chain management. A key question is, why have efforts to improve forecasting failed? It should be noted that most forecasting measures deal with improving forecasting error, not necessarily improving forecasting procedure and technique. In order to generate an accurate forecast, the planning process must be dramatically improved to build on relevant information and engage the appropriate players.

The business planning process typically begins in marketing. Marketing forecasts and plans target sale of product, which fulfills a sales and profit estimate supporting financial projections shared with Wall Street. The forecast then moves to sales administration, where it is allocated geographically and field sales objectives are assigned, depending upon sales force structure and classes of trade serviced. Field sales has to assign the forecast, customer specific, and determine if the planned merchandising and promotional programs are sufficient to support expectations.

At the same time, an operational forecast is developed to drive operations planning. This forecast is typically generated using a model to generate product production plans and make assignments to the right location. There is typically more than a bit of disconnect between the marketing/sales forecast and the operational forecast. Keeping in mind this forecast disconnect, the plan still must synergize with the customer's planning cycle. Unless the plan locks in with the customer's plans, the window of opportunity will not exist.

There are informational and planning gaps that exist when developing a comprehensive business plan designed to achieve both sales and marketing objectives, result in an efficient and effective supply chain, and delight the consumer. The challenge is to determine how to improve the process and information flow using existing technology.

The first step in breaking the existing paradigm is to bring the trading partners together in a collaborative planning initiative designed to exchange information and marketing intelligence in an effort to develop a marketing-specific forecast. Secondarily, there must be collaboration within companies, for example, between sales and marketing, logistics and operations, ad third-party service providers, as well as customers and suppliers.

Next, a process and system to support the plan that facilitates easy and ready exchange of actionable information is essential. Finally, the use of existing communication standards, capable of linking value-added activities in the supply chain, is essential. To facilitate communication, earlier applications of collaborative planning and forecasting have been based on internet information exchange. All of the steps listed above will only become reality if driven by effective leadership.

5. Reminiscences of Days Gone By

For those of us in logistics and supply chain, Nabisco was a great place to work despite the turmoil and uncertainty associated with all the mergers and acquisitions that occurred in the 1980s. We supported and helped each other, and strong relationships—not just on the business side but also friendships—were formed. Many of us have stayed in touch, and we hold an informal Nabisco alumni reunion each year during the Council of Supply Chain Management Professionals annual conference. I reached out to some of my former colleagues and asked them to contribute some of their memories for this book. Their recollections will clearly show how special our group was, and what a unique culture we all shared. Whether or not you ever worked for Nabisco, I think you'll enjoy them.

My career began with Nabisco, working for Gerry Cantwell. I was as naïve as they come … and I know some of you would attest to that! From day 1, I felt a trust in my management team, had loyal friends at work, and built lasting relationships, most of which I still have today! There are numerous reasons Nabisco was a great place to work. (I laughed every day … well almost every day!)

1) Relationship building: The company was small enough that you were able to get to know many people, and not just in supply chain.
2) Genuine people: I had numerous people I could trust and confide in; my managers genuinely cared what I was doing, how I was doing, and my career path. Hell, Rob even gave me marriage advice …
3) Strong work ethic: I could count on the reliability of my teammates on projects and in daily business execution.
4) Friendly competition: We all had the desire to succeed and do well but supported each other along the way.

5) Succession planning: This helped to define our career paths, communicate about our people, and mentor and coach those highlighted as needing an extra "push" to succeed. We planned for the future to ensure we had new recruits in from top colleges, like Penn State, and had teams to recruit from key universities each year. So often today I find companies are behind the game in recruiting talent.

6) Communication of a strong vision, objectives, and priorities: Joe, Rick, and Paul all created a strong vision that resonated through the team and cascaded into our objectives. We knew what we had to do to be successful every day, and the leadership was dynamic.

7) Team-building activities (work hard/play hard): Now this is an area where I have a lot of FOND memories!! We had so many good times together, whether it was Rookie Night, dancing and drinking, deep-sea fishing, Vegas sales meetings, Vermont ski trips, basketball games after work with Rob Wodarczyk, Marty Baum, John Williamson, etc.; softball games with Cheryl Simechek, Tony Bruno, and Kim Brong, etc. ... such great memories!!

I am amazed by the systems and processes we had more than 20 years ago that today, I can still NOT get with SAP, Oracle, etc. We had the IT team that saw the vision of supply chain vs. trying to shove a system in that was not truly supply chain-oriented. Amazes me every day (where is the ON81, the ON45, the ON20E??? We had Steve Cortese build us the load-builder report with Shri Amrute—remember??? Why is this so difficult? We made the complex, easy. Period.

I still have copies of all of my reviews. I have a copy of the famous Al Yasalonis MIRROR report that was a bear to put together (thank goodness for Chrissy Gallagher), and he drove Steve Hard and I nuts. But we learned a lot ... at least that's what we told ourselves!

I have been supported throughout my career by some of the most successful logisticians in companies across the U.S.—Rick, Paul, Debbie, Rob, Al, Tracy, Cory, Debbie, Gemma, Mary, Gerry, Steve, Agnes, Dingley, Jeff Cowan, and on and on ... and some of my best friends, who are still in my life today! (Girl's night out with Tracy, Gemma, and Shilpa!!, Chicago trip with Cory, Julie Weix, Debbie Weishaar, and a crazy taxi driver!) The stories still go on! I love you guys!!

How were we able to succeed and make progress amid the turmoil and constant change caused by mergers and acquisitions? We always put our best foot forward, head down, and came up with a plan and executed. We had an organization that gave us autonomy to "go" to create a plan and move forward. As examples, we were given the challenges of closing a plant from a planning perspective and managing the inventory planning integration for Farley Sathers, and did what we had to do. We had the talent to execute and the team to conquer it. We had a lot of change but I guess that growing up with it, it taught me that one thing is constant, and that is change. We had a desire to succeed and not let the team—or the new team—down.

How were we able to create collaborative relationships with the operating companies, carriers, and distribution centers? We broke down the traditional barriers that exist between corporate and field operations. We listened to their needs, they were part of our success, and we were a team. We traveled to their locations and listened to them. Debbie Mee and Ralph Vasquez at Oxnard were tough cookies, but after a while, we worked well together. We learned how to work with different people with different agendas and objectives, and we learned how to find a common ground.

> —*Karen Moller, Director, Commercialization Planning, Campbell Soup*

Favorite memory of the Nabisco days? I'm not sure I can think of one memory, but as a whole, the biggest sensation and feeling I got from working with Nabisco was the partnership. I believe the word "partnership" is used a lot in business but true partnerships don't happen as much as the word is used. I spent at least a decade working with Nabisco, and while many of those years I might have been too far removed from top management to feel some of the hardships of a relationship, what I did feel throughout that time was a true sense of mutual responsibility and quest to improve. I definitely felt the push and drive to be better and continuously improve. We got kicked in the butt but it felt like we were in the trenches together. There was support, education, and praise when things went right. The exposure to best practices, 1,000-point audits, customer visits, and seeing all sides of the supply chain were priceless. There was no better way to learn our industry and no better education than working with the Nabisco group.

I couldn't have accomplished what I have so far without the education and learning I've gained from all the folks I've worked with and partnered with. The Nabisco crew were second to none! Bruce Montgomery was one in particular. In 1996, I had one of the first opportunities to speak at a conference and I couldn't have done it without Bruce's support ... I was incredibly nervous. You've raised some truly great folks, Joe! Including giving me the nickname "Grasshopper!"

—W. Ryan Donovan, Vice President, Operations & Business Development, States Logistics Services Inc.

In late 1975, I had been promoted to Director of Industrial Relations for the Grocery Division. The division had margarine plants in Dallas, Texas; Oakland, Calif.; Indianapolis, Ind.; and Pennsauken, N.J. There were also coffee plants in Chicago, New Orleans, and Hoboken, N.J. Our only non-union facility was Pennsauken, and it was not doing very well. Al Spindler was the plant manager. The year before the Amalgamated Meat Cutters Union had filed a petition to unionize the plant and had lost the election by three votes. This and many other issues with the division had resulted in Bob Schaedler being recruited to head up manufacturing for the Grocery Division.

Since we were getting many complaints from Pennsauken, Bob decided (with prompting from Bob Carbonell) that the management team should head down to Pennsauken and find out what was going on. It soon became obvious that the management team at Pennsauken had totally lost control of the facility. They were so scared of it going union that they had lost any semblance of management, and it was obvious that there was very little respect for the team. As one of the more popular/respected production workers (Peanut) advised me, "Mr. Spindler is a very nice man but if you don't get him out of here we are doomed." In addition, he advised that the people hated the personnel manager.

Bob Schaedler proved to be a man of action, and after our meetings down there he advised me that I needed to recruit a whole new team. This took a few months, but one Thursday we visited the facility and advised the old team they were history and the next day introduced the new team to the employees. Luckily, as plant manager we had recruited Richard Sterling, and he was the perfect individual for this assignment. Within a few weeks he and his new team began to make progress. When I again visited the plant it was obvious there was a different atmosphere and that most people not only liked Rich but respected him.

However, despite this we soon received another petition from the NLRB re the Amalgamated Meat Cutters effort to organize the Pennsauken plant. After a meeting with all the parties on May 4, 1976, it was agreed the election would occur on June 3. Henry Weigl became involved and made it clear that we'd better not lose the election. While we thought we were doing better since the previous election was so close, no one was betting we would win this one, as many workers felt they should give the union a chance, and if it didn't work they could always go back to non-union. We in management knew this would be a disaster.

So with Rich in control we ran a campaign based on giving management one more chance. We held listening meetings to develop an idea of the issues, but while we could indicate that we heard all the problems we could not promise anything, and the union could promise the world. However, Rich had really made a difference, and the people for the first time in a while believed Pennsauken had a future. On June 1, we had our final meetings with small groups. I explained in detail the vote proceedings to give the people, especially the new ones, a real understanding of how everything would work during and after the vote. Then Rich gave a very effective short talk.

The vote wasn't close, and the employees voted 90 to 44 against the union. It was a great victory for Rich and his team and showed how in a short period of time a new management team can turn things around. Mr. Weigl was sure his threats were the key, but as someone else stated, "Sometimes you need to hit bottom to get a good fix!"

—Howard Pines, Co-founder and Chairman, BeamPines Inc.

I still look forward to the Nabisco reunion at CSCMP every year. It has been 20 years since I was at Nabisco. The Nabisco team continues to be thought of as friends, and I enjoy seeing everyone and hearing about where they are. That team has ended up in different businesses across the nation and it is exciting to hear how successful everyone is!

As recently as last month, I shared with the Dannon supply chain team the importance of involvement in industry. Dannon has many young professionals that we are encouraging to get involved in CSCMP and now SCPro. I told them of my experience with Nabisco and in particular its leader—you!—who enthusiastically encouraged us to "get involved" and be leaders with best practices. I was able to work with transportation leaders to develop EDI standards and lead the industry to implement EDI, even to speaking at CSCMP while I was in my 20s! Since then

I have been involved with many industry organizations and have contacts throughout the industry that I depend on and share best practices with. I attribute the start of that to your encouragement!!

Funny stories that I still share with people:

One day while I was National Transportation Manager you stood in front of my cube. You had several people around you. You drew an imaginary line with your foot saying that one side was positive and one side negative. You then began to jump (and I mean jump!) from the negative to the positive, stating that it was each person's decision and to get with it (I'm paraphrasing). Being positive is a choice! Jump into the positive! You were such an inspiration.

My cube was along the wall with the path between your office at one end and I believe Sales at the other end. Many times you were so charged up that you could not walk from one end to the other. I would hear you running by! At first I used to stand and look. But over time, I would just sit at my desk and smile. Such energy!

> —*Diane Van Wagner, Director, Distribution & Transportation Operations, The Dannon Company*

The year was 1985; seems like a lifetime ago, and it really was. I had just been named Region Manager for the west for the Nabisco warehouse businesses, including the soon-to-be-added RJR Del Monte Brands. I was just 30 years old, and my fellow RMs around the country were all under the age of 32. Amazing that the national business was placed in the hands of a team of people so young.

With that came the need for more learning and experience in many facets of the business, of which one was Integrated Logistics. Most of my career at that time was made up of calling on customers, selling programs and taking orders and then thinking the job was done, but I quickly learned it really had just started. It was a time when customers and our own company started to realize that the cost of too much or too little inventory was extraordinary. Interest rates were 5-fold what they are today, so there was a need to improve the sales and logistics model to maintain or lower costs.

What that meant for Sales was the need to engage other functional teams in the organization, especially Logistics, to be sure we had the right product at the right time in the right place. In many ways Joe and his team led and held hands with the Sales team in sharing and creating an improved and very open line of communication that led to better service to our customers. Being out west with many of our manufacturing facilities located in the east made my team's job all the more important.

Long story short, together we created one of the better S&IL organizations in the food industry. Joe and team in many cases tried new and different approaches to try to reduce our costs to land product in our customers' facilities at the very best cost. It worked and prospered for many years—so well, I guess, that since that time Nabisco has been gobbled up by larger companies or investment bankers at least three times, at a premium each time. They must have liked what they saw.

It was a great time, in fact maybe the best time to grow up in this business. I worked with great people who became great friends. It was like a big family.

Thanks for the great memories.

> —*John J. Flack, Customer Vice President, Mondelez International*

There were several factors that contributed to the Nabisco culture that made it such a great place to learn and grow. Promote from within, aggressive pursuit of new talent from top logistics schools, an expectation of several lateral moves within the various logistics areas and company regions, competitive environment, and a requirement to have managed an operating area like a warehouse prior to major advancement.

However, for me, the one aspect that stuck and kept me interested was the support and promotion of constant innovation, development, and risk taking. Whether it was the development of a bar-coded RF warehouse management system, a new network configuration, testing a new intermodal technology, or the development of an inventory tracking system, all departments were expected to innovate. These were the activities and experiences that stretched the imagination and left indelible impressions on me and have assisted me throughout my career.

> —*Greg Sargis, President, Gem State Logistics and LOGO Carriers*

Teamwork. Partnership. Collaboration. Just words for some, but for those of us lucky enough to be a part of the Nabisco management team in the 1990s, those words embodied the spirit of both who we were and how we worked within our company and with our customers. Twenty years later, companies are still working to perfect the concepts and business models pioneered within Nabisco's Sales & Integrated Logistics organization. These included collaborative planning and forecasting, automatic replenishment, cost-to-serve models, logistics efficiency pricing ... just to name a few.

I would just like to say thanks to my S&IL teammates for allowing me to be a part of that team, and a special thank you to Joe Andraski ... for his vision, leadership, courage, and commitment to excellence. Joe, you made it all possible. Only looking back now do I understand just what a gift I was being given.

> —*Darin Cooprider, Vice President and General Manager, Ryder System Inc.*

I began my supply chain career in an entry-level position at Nabisco Brands as an inventory analyst, not realizing how fortunate I would be to learn from the best in the business. The office environment was electric, full of high energy, hard-charging young leaders eager to make a difference—not only to meet the challenging demands of Nabisco's foodservice and grocery retail customers but also to further their own ambitious career development plans. The team knew how to work hard and how to play hard, and many life-long friendships were established.

As the corporate leader of this hard-charging group, Joe Andraski set the pace for the entire group. He had the unique ability to balance a nurturing style with a commanding presence, always driving for excellence for himself and for others. A style that many try to imitate but few are able to duplicate.

I feel grateful that I had the chance to begin my career with such a premier supply chain organization. It established a tremendous foundation for me—a foundation of learning and experience that I will always value.

> —*Jim Lawrence, Chief Supply Chain Officer, Darden Restaurants*

I was just talking to a co-worker the other day about how it is so difficult in today's workplace to build the level of teamwork we had in the

SBI/NBI days. The things we did, like Rookie Night, were great growth and team-building activities for young employees growing in the management program, where people couldn't "hide" in anonymity as they do today. Today's business culture that supports quickly oppressed and offended employees who take themselves more seriously than their work has made it much less fun to go to work, and much less productive when the chips are down and a result must be achieved. What's in it for me? It's a function of the times, and things that developed employees in the past are considered bullying today. Many of today's employees could not care less whether or not a key customer's need is met, and despite the tools and technology available to employees today, the Nabisco team was able to adapt, improvise, and overcome to meet any customer need more effectively than today's employee.

I remember that the bar was always set high. Zero defects. Zero shipped/unbilled at quarter end. It wasn't okay to get a result that didn't meet the objectives, and people wanted to help each other achieve their complete objectives, even across the regional customer service centers.

    —*Vince Livingston, Executive Director, Operations, Motor Coach Industries*

This is a long and humorous story that almost no one at SBI knew. In fact I can recall only four or five people who were involved in it besides me. It's the saga of the introduction of the Reggie Candy Bar at Yankee Stadium in 1978. What I'm about to write is absolutely true. Unfortunately, there may not be anyone else to verify it—except maybe Jackson himself, if he remembers what happened.

Reggie Jackson (from now on I'll just use RJ) had said when he wasn't playing for the Yankees, "If I played in New York they would name a candy bar for me."

When he became a Yankee he was also a spokesman for products produced by Standard Brands. SBI had a candy division in Chicago called Curtiss Candy, which produced Baby Ruth and Butterfingers candy bars. Someone at SBI thought that it would be a wonderful idea to in fact produce a candy bar and name it for RJ. And so the Reggie Bar concept was born.

Despite the fact that the Yankees' colors are blue and white, the Reggie bars were made with an orange and blue wrapper, which are the colors of New York City and coincidently the colors of the Yankees' rival team in Queens, the New York Mets. You can bet no Yankees fans, such as me,

174

were consulted beforehand! The candy bar was made in Ft. Wayne, Ind., by Wayne Candies, probably because they already produced similar round chocolate bars called Wayne Buns.

So in 1978 I was sitting in my office when I received a phone call from the Reggie Bar product manager, which went something like the following:

PM: Hank, I want you to ship a truckload of Reggie Bars to Yankee Stadium for Sunday's game. We're going to give away the bars and introduce them at the game.

HG (me): I can't do that.

PM: Why not?

HG: Because they haven't passed quality control inspection.

PM: But we're introducing the bar at the game.

HG: Sorry, no QC approval, no shipment.

15 minutes later I got another call—this time from the VP of Marketing.

VP: Hank, I understand you have a problem.

HG: I don't have a problem. You have a problem.

VP: We must have that candy at the stadium for Sunday's game.

HG: I can't ship them without QC approval.

VP: Ship them now without their approval.

HG: I won't do it.

Fifteen minutes later there was yet another call, this time from the VP of Sales. Same dialogue, same results.

Fifteen minutes after that, Jim Marler, the president of the consumer products division, calls me. Now Jim was a man of integrity who I admired and respected very much.

JM: Hank, I understand we have a problem.

HG: We do, Jim. Sales and Marketing wants me to move Reggie Bars from Wayne to Yankee Stadium without QC approval.

JM: Hank, it's okay to move them. I'll take the responsibility.

And with his assurance and blessing I authorized the shipment.

Now we come to the humorous part of the story.

As each fan gave his or her ticket at entrance he or she was handed a Reggie Bar in a nice orange and blue wrapper with a picture of Reggie Jackson hitting a baseball.

At his first time at bat Reggie hits a home run, and as he is rounding third base to go home all the fans on the left field side of the stadium threw their Reggie Bars on the field.

And there I was, 50 miles away, watching the game on TV in my living room and smiling.

And that, my friend, is a true story.

—Hank Gallitano, President, Distribution Consulting Associates

The '80s were truly the golden years at Nabisco. The late, great Andy Yuhas once said, "Setting the pace, not keeping the pace—that's what it is all about." Although Andy's commentary was related to the Planter's Pacesetter program, it reflected the can-do winning spirit of the S&L team led by John Murray and Bob Magrann. These two sales leaders set the tone, successfully motivating the troops to deliver year after year outstanding sales performances.

—John Ferramosca, Partner, Edgewood Consulting Group

Being a member of the Nabisco Logistics team clearly was a highlight of my career—one of the very rare opportunities to be part of a professional family that worked as a truly unified team. We had intense loyalty for each other, with strong bonds and high motivation to achieve phenomenal results. And we did! We truly achieved breakthroughs and were innovative, and were highly valued by our customers and business partners. Without a doubt, a testimony of great leadership, high

176

expectations and performance (yes ... dress-right-dress, Joe!),
and strong relationships that have continued over a decade later.

—Debbie Lentz, Senior Vice President Customer Service & Logistics, Kraft Foods Group

You have had an impact on my vocational life and also my personal life. You provided great leadership, teaching, wisdom, and inspiration. You went out of your way and broadened my business and emotional intelligence. In reflection, you were someone I looked up to in many ways. Our times at Nabisco were very special and produced many everlasting memories and lifelong learnings.

—Tom Moeller, Executive Vice President, FTD Inc.

You developed a structure and facilitated teamwork where the team brought Supply Chain from a "necessary department" to a "competitive advantage." Your dedication and diligence to ensuring S&IL made each of us determined to not let you or the company down. I think of spending the Thanksgiving holiday in 1986 working in the Dallas office researching where recalled cases of Baby Ruth Bars were shipped. Not thinking twice about missing holiday time, but rather focusing on finding every last case to ensure we could prove we ran a tight ship. I'm sure that was the same thought for all the other folks in the other regions as well. It was our job, and you instilled in us that we were only as good as other departments and our customers perceived us to be. I think we met and in fact surpassed others' expectations.

—William Bock, Executive Vice President of Logistics, Haas Group

Nabisco Foods ... from the view of a field salesperson during the '80s and '90s.

Having confidence in your organization from top to bottom is a critical element in creating long-term profitable growth. From my viewpoint in field sales, Nabisco Foods Group and its Sales & Distribution arm had terrific management from the top throughout the organization.

Throughout the 1980s and well into the '90s, Nabisco Foods was an exciting place to be for a sales guy. We had a very competitive organization that was built to succeed and driven to do so. Our management challenged us to explore all avenues in which to place our products for consumers to see and purchase. We had lofty goals

177

and were pushed to exceed all expectations. In order to expand product placement, we relied heavily on our Supply Chain Group.

As part of the non-grocery sales unit, we sold directly to every imaginable place and avenue. And I mean every place … from K-mart, Wal-Mart, Walgreens, and Woolworth stores (remember them?) to vending operators, stadiums, military bases, and yes, even prisons. I can tell many a story about walking down the halls of a minimum-security women's prison located just outside of Lexington, Ky., as a 26-year-old. Those ladies sure had some interesting things they wanted to do to and with me!

We also were part of a group of snack and candy manufacturers that convinced the new up-and-coming office supply retailers (Office Depot, Staples, and OfficeMax) that adding consumables to their offerings made smart business sense. I can honestly say that these times were the best of my and many others' careers. We were afforded the opportunity and flexibility to succeed and were rewarded accordingly.

None of this success could have happened without our supply chain partners. There were many sacrifices and less-than-profitable decisions made in order to support our business development efforts. Drop-shipping LTL orders all over the country is not something that many of our competitors could or would consider doing. Hell, I can recall many quarter-end periods where we shipped as little as 15 cases of Planters nuts to virtually every Kmart, Wal-Mart, and Walgreens in the country … and our supply chain made it happen!

Our Sales and Logistics groups were a great group of professionals and all focused on the same goals: exceed assigned objectives and kick the shit out of the competition … which we did. Oh, and we all had a good time along the way. Field Sales was led by Don "Dewar's and a splash of water" Marler, one hell of a guy! We all miss Don. God bless, and ROOOOOLLLLLL TIDE. Our Supply Chain group was led by Joe "Poppa" Andraski, and he made it all happen. What great memories I have of these many years and of the many everlasting and cherished friendships that developed.

—*Steve Haverly, Customer Business Lead, Mondelez International*

I'm working in project management training and thought of you, Joe, when hearing this: "Long after people forget your words, they will remember how you made them feel." Thanks for being a great leader and mentor. You always made me feel needed and appreciated.

—Dan Mattas, Business Excellence Manager, Harsco Corp.

"Collaborative Energizer" might be the name of his company, but it is also an apt description of the man himself—Joe Andraski. I have had the pleasure of knowing Joe for the better part of 10 years, and his passion, vision, and non-stop championing of retail supply chain enhancements through ideation, innovation, standards, best practices, and implementation are legendary. He is a recognized spokesperson for the industry with an insatiable appetite for the supply chain. I have benefited greatly from our time together. Joe is certainly an industry ambassador, but more than that, he is a friend to all those who share the same passion to drive supply chain solutions.

—Steve Matheys, Executive Vice President, Chief Administrative Officer, Schneider National

One of my favorite thoughts about leadership is "Great leaders inspire ordinary people to do extraordinary things." They create the environment and blaze the trail so that success is increasingly achievable. This is not accomplished in a single moment in time, but rather, over one's career. You may not know it or see it when it's happening, but when you look back, the picture is clear. Joe is that leader. The indelible imprint he has had on our discipline is remarkable, yet the individuals who have had the great fortune of working with and knowing Joe have been impacted to an even greater degree. Most are terrific leaders, imparting much of what they learned from Joe to another generation of future supply chain leaders, helping to ensure this great profession continues to grow in its value and contribution to the world we live in. On behalf of a grateful discipline, Joe, we thank you and are honored to know you!

—Rick Blasgen, President & CEO, Council of Supply Chain Management Professionals

In Chapter 2, I included some reminiscences from Peter N. Rogers, former president of Nabisco Foods and several other divisions of Standard Brands and Nabisco. Peter was kind enough to send in many amazing tales about his days working under Henry Weigl, who was CEO of Standard Brands for 20 years, and F. Ross Johnson, the president of Standard Brands who was behind the merger with Nabisco and later the Nabisco-R.J. Reynolds merger. Johnson became president and CEO of RJR Nabisco. Here are more of his stories:

In my "prime," just before RJR, I could sign purchase orders up to $10 million, while in Henry Weigl's days, he reviewed every salary above $25K and would delay an increase by two months just to save a penny or two!

My first personal involvement with Henry was in 1971. Even though I was based in Canada, Henry appointed me to represent Standard Brands (SBI) on the Grocery Manufacturers of America (GMA) bar-code (UPC) committee. This way he had me report directly to him on this project. I suspect that he wanted to use me as a spy to report on the activities of one Ross Johnson, because he always brought Ross's name into every conversation. He was appalled when I reported that one of the implications of the UPC was that inventories would be transferred from customer warehouses to manufacturer warehouses, and/or we would need to build regional manufacturing plants.

Weigl taught me to evaluate certain expenses in cases or packages of product. "Peter, how many additional packages of Fleischmann's yeast do we need to sell in order to give your secretary a 5-percent salary increase?" Sounds silly, but it came in useful when I was running a company in Chapter 11 bankruptcy for three years.

I took over Curtiss Candy in August 1973 and made my first budget presentation to Henry in November. Things did not start well when I opened my presentation at 10 a.m. with a statement that I thought that SBI should divest the Curtiss business. (Henry had acquired Curtiss.) The presentation lasted until 7:15 p.m. Henry had a sandwich for lunch, and I was offered NOTHING.

After nine hours, Henry said, "I enjoyed sparring with you Peter. No one around here ever stands up to me like you did." He then asked how he should set earnings targets for the division presidents and how he should handle the budget process. I told him that he should accept nothing less than an increase in earnings that was 3 percent above the rate of inflation. In other words, if inflation is 5 percent, then he should expect an increase in earnings of 8 percent.

He was ecstatic, turned round on Mazda, (our name for Chuck Walker, the CFO, because when nervous he would hum like the new rotary-engine Mazda car), shouted at him, calling him damned useless and telling him to make sure that this directive went out to all divisions before morning.

180

He then clapped me on the shoulder, walked me to the street, told me to have dinner at Delmonico's, cancel my flight back to Chicago, and be in his office at 9 a.m. the next day, when he made a personal bet with me that I would not be able to successfully integrate Curtiss with Planters non-grocery by April 1, 1974. (YES, he chose All Fool's Day).

Curtiss operated on a 13 x four-week accounting year while Planters operated on a calendar-month basis; there were all kinds of issues with customer numbers, order forms, and product codes; there was the need to open consolidated warehouse operations, etc., etc. BUT we were successful, and he gave me a bottle of Black & White scotch and was very glowing in his praise because he thought that Jack Baker and Bill Malloy would fight me. But I moved Jack and Bill to Chicago (although Bill always kept a house in Pa.), made them co-conspirators, and gave them something to lose—like a job AFTER they had relocated.

Henry then decided that I was senior management material and asked that I personally hire my replacement. I had to fly to NYC twice a month. On one occasion we were down to résumés of three candidates. Henry asked for a thumbnail on each person. I ranked them in order of preference but said of the top recommendation that I thought that he was a little young for the job (he was 42) because the candy industry was complex by class-of-trade, etc. Henry leant back in his chair and absolutely roared with laughter. "Peter, do you realize what you just said?" I replied that I thought that candidate A was too young and that we needed to look further. "Peter, exactly how old are YOU?" "Thirty-seven," I replied. "Peter, I rest my case."

Shortly thereafter Henry was replaced, but when I met him in Palm Beach on his 90th birthday, he reminded me of the occasion.

One time when Ross Johnson and I were touring Canada, he said, "NEVER, ever build a warehouse." When I asked why, he replied, "Because if you do, sure as shit someone will put product in it and you'll destroy your balance sheet and cash flow. There'll always be a few railcars or rental space if you need it, but NEVER, ever build a warehouse!"

Ross's approach to "sharing the candy" was not totally altruistic, as is exemplified by a cartoon with the chairman of a company addressing 10 managers seated around a table. The caption read: "I know that you can't buy loyalty, but at least it can be rented!"

On the other hand, here is a personal anecdote that illustrates Ross's very pragmatic approach to compensation. In 1971, after I became responsible for the newly constituted Confectionery Division, I decided to terminate the president of Moirs Chocolates, which was based in Halifax, Nova Scotia, a remote location. Ross asked what I intended to give him as severance pay, and I told him three months.

Ross asked, "Why so little?"

I replied, "Well, he's only been here for three years." Remember, one month per year of service was the norm in 1971.

Ross then said, "Rook, here's your first lesson. I suspect that Charlie is not the only person that you will terminate during the restructuring, and I further suspect that you will be actively hiring some 'Young Turks.' IF you treat terminated employees in a miserly fashion, none of the Young Turks will come to work for you. Remember my boy, Canada is a small country, and the business community is relatively smaller because we are in part a branch-plant economy."

Charlie was paid $35K—not bad in those days in a low-cost area like Nova Scotia.

The three months would have been taxable income, so Ross suggested the following: Give him a $15K tax-free relocation allowance (worth $22K before taxes); $3K in tax-free outplacement counseling (worth $4K pre-tax), and THEN give him four months' pay paid out over eight months. This will approximate a year's salary, and you will give him some income for an eight-month period rather than a three-month lump sum. AND don't forget that he is a 56-year-old executive who is being fired by a 33-year-old "punk," so give him some bragging rights! MOST EXCELLENT ADVICE.

—*Peter Rogers, former President, Nabisco Brands*

6. Glossary

This glossary of some of the terms used in the book was contributed by my dear friend and Nabisco colleague Al Yasalonis. I hope you'll find it helpful.

4GL (Fourth-Generation Language)
4GLs are designed to reduce programming effort, the time it takes to develop software, and the cost of software development.

ARTIST (Adhoc Reports Transportation Information Support Tool)
The first tool at Nabisco that allowed transportation analysts to gain ad hoc, selective analysis of global freight payment data. Front-end user interface screens allowed users to pick selective dates, ship points, carriers, and even rate proposal differentials.

COBAL (Common Business Oriented Language)
One of the oldest programming languages, defining its primary domain in business, finance, and administrative systems for companies and governments. COBOL alienated Nabisco's logistics analysts and drove them toward the 4GLs like Nomad, which enabled more reporting visibility.

CRM (Customer Relationship Management)
General term for customer relationship systems, data collection, and information flows.

CSCMP (Council of Supply Chain Management Professionals)
A global supply chain professional organization. Its CEO, Rick Blasgen, is a Nabisco alumnus.

DCMS (Distribution Center Management System)
A term coined by Nabisco and Trammell Crow in the 1980s. DCMS is an enterprise-oriented application designed to track the activities performed in a distribution center (DC) and to provide automated solutions for all the operations needed for efficient functioning and accurate financial reporting.

DOCS (Distribution Operations Control System)
System used to monitor on-time delivery date performance across multiple company regions.

Fax Gate (Fax software used to collect DOCS info [see DOCS])
Used by regional offices to disseminate and collect daily order details that were missing, such as actual delivery date performance.

FMI (Food Marketing Institute)
An international organization that conducts food safety, public affairs, education, research, and industry relations programs for food retailers and wholesalers.

GMA (Grocery Manufacturers Association)
The world's largest trade association representing the food, beverage, and consumer products industry.

GS1
A neutral, not-for-profit, international organization that develops and maintains standards for supply and demand chains across multiple sectors. Its standards include those for bar codes, electronic product codes, global data synchronization, and radio frequency identification (RFID). Regional organizations (such as GS1 US) administer the GS1 system of standards and provide education and support.

GTIN (Global Trade Identification Number)
Unique, universal identifier for trade items developed by GS1 (including those from the former EAN International and Uniform Code Council, among others). The identifier is useful in establishing which product in one database corresponds to which product in another database, especially across organizational boundaries.

ILRFID (Item-Level Radio Frequency Identification)
Item-level, wireless, non-contact use of radio-frequency electromagnetic fields to transfer data, for the purposes of automatically identifying and tracking tags attached to objects.

KKR (Kohlberg Kravis Roberts & Company)
U.S. multinational private equity firm specializing in leveraged buyouts. The firm, now known as KKR & Co., sponsors and manages private equity investment funds. It acquired RJR Nabisco in 1988.

LBO (Leveraged Buyout)
The purchase of a company or single asset with a combination of equity plus significant amounts of borrowed money, structured in such a way that the target's cash flows or assets are used as the collateral ("leverage") to secure and repay the money borrowed to make the purchase.

LITS (Logistics Inventory Tracking System)
Gathered hundreds of Inventory Management System fields across past daily inventory balance and/or exception reports from Nabisco proprietary systems to relationally connect data details.

LOTS (Logistics Order Tracking System)
Gathered hundreds of Order Management System fields to relationally connect data details. LOTS also included relational product and customer master data fields for all item/stock-keeping units and customer and operational ship-to data elements.

MIRROR (Manufacturing, Investment, Replenishment, Reporting, Order Fulfillment, and Reverse Logistics)
Included reflective data on supply chain metrics, primarily for the divergent Specialty Products Division. MIRROR had over 24 specific metrics within the categories reflected in the acronym.

NOMAD (NCSS Owned, Maintained, and Developed)
Relational database and fourth-generation language (4GL), originally developed in the 1970s by time-sharing vendor National CSS Inc. While it is still in use today, its widest use was in the '70s and '80s.

OMS (Order Management System)
Software system used in a number of industries for order entry and processing.

PRIDE (Personal Radio Input Device Education)
Beta-level system tied to radio frequency (RF) device training in the earliest days of warehouse management systems (WMS) and RF-based implementations.

RF (Radio Frequency)
Radio signals sent to centralized servers in the warehouse, used to transmit data encoded in bar codes from bar-code readers or scanners to those computers for further order management or warehouse transactions.

RJR (R.J. Reynolds Industries)
Merged with Nabisco Brands in 1985, changing its name to RJR Nabisco in 1986. In 1988, the private equity takeover firm Kohlberg Kravis Roberts & Company conducted a leveraged buyout of RJR Nabisco. This was documented in the bestselling book, Barbarians at the Gate: The Fall of RJR Nabisco, and later a made-for-television movie.

S&IL (Sales & Integrated Logistics)
Nabisco's sales and logistics organizations were combined under the leadership of the president of S&IL, with vice presidents heading up Sales and Logistics individually.

S&OP (Sales & Operations Planning)
Collaborative method of coordinating key forecasting and related operational functions across cash-to-cash supply chain activities.

SBI (Standard Brands Inc.)
Manufacturer of such brands as Fleischmann, Planters, Curtiss Candy, and other food products. Merged with Nabisco in 1981 to form Nabisco Brands Inc.

SCM (Supply Chain Management)
The management of interconnected networks, channels, and nodes in businesses providing products and services to customers. It has been defined as the "design, planning, execution, control, and monitoring of supply chain activities with the objective of creating net value, building a competitive infrastructure, leveraging worldwide logistics, synchronizing supply with demand and measuring performance globally." SCM draws heavily from the areas of operations management, logistics, procurement, and information technology, and strives for an integrated approach.

TMS (Transportation Management System)
Software used to suggest routing solutions for inbound and outbound orders, among other tasks. Once the best provider is selected, the solution typically generates electronic load tendering and track/trace to execute the optimized shipment with the selected carrier, and later to support freight audit and payment. Links back to enterprise resource planning (ERP) systems and sometimes to warehouse management (WMS) programs linked to the ERP.

TQM (Total Quality Management)
Management philosophy based on the premise that the quality of products and processes is the responsibility of everyone involved with the creation or consumption of the products or services offered by an organization. Requires the involvement of management, workforce, suppliers, and customers.

VICS (Voluntary Interindustry Commerce Solutions Association)
Retail-focused organization, merged in 2012 with GS1 US and the Apparel and General Merchandise Initiative, as a single "clearinghouse" for the development of standards, guidelines, and best practices that can be incorporated into retail business processes.

VM 370/CMS (Virtual Machine -Cambridge Monitor System)
Developed by IBM in the early 1970s. Used by Nabisco's supply chain group in the mid-1980s. Ran on a mainframe but its interactive environment is comparable to that of a single-user PC, including a file system, programming services, device access, and command-line processing.

WERC (Warehousing Education and Research Council)
Professional association offering educational events, performance metrics for benchmarking, research, expert insights, and peer-to-peer knowledge exchange for distribution and warehousing professionals.

WMS (Warehouse Management System)
Software that primarily aims to control the movement and storage of materials within a warehouse and process the associated transactions, including shipping, receiving, putaway, and picking. It involves the physical warehouse infrastructure, tracking systems, and communication between product stations.

Made in the USA
Lexington, KY
20 January 2017